around WASHINGTON, D.C.

WITHDRAWN with KIDS

by Kathryn McKay

6th EDITION

FODOR'S TRAVEL PUBLICATIONS

New York ✳ Toronto ✳ London ✳ Sydney ✳ Auckland

www.fodors.com

Credits

Writer: Kathryn McKay

Editor: Jennifer DePrima
Editorial Production: Carolyn Roth
Production Manager: Steve Slawsky

Design: Fabrizio La Rocca, *creative director*;
Nora Rosansky, *art director*
Cover Art and Design: Jessie Hartland
Flip Art and Illustration: Rico Lins, Keren Ora
Admoni/Rico Lins Studio

About the Writer

Writer Kathryn McKay covers a lot of ground, but her favorite place to write about is her hometown, Washington, D.C. She travels frequently with her two children and their nine cousins.

Sixth Edition
ISBN: 978-1-4000-0517-8
ISSN: 1526-1980

Important Tip

Although all prices, opening times, and other details in this book are based on information supplied to us as of this writing, changes occur all the time in the travel world, and Fodor's cannot accept responsibility for facts that become outdated or for inadvertent errors or omissions. So always confirm information when it matters, especially if you're making a detour to visit a specific place.

Special Sales

This book is available at special discounts for bulk purchases for sales promotions or premiums. Special editions, including personalized covers, excerpts of existing books, and corporate imprints, can be created in large quantities for special needs. For more information, write to Special Markets/Premium Sales, 1745 Broadway, MD 6-2, New York, NY 10019, or e-mail specialmarkets@randomhouse.com.

PRINTED IN THE UNITED STATES OF AMERICA
10 9 8 7 6 5 4 3 2 1

COUNTDOWN TO GOOD TIMES

GET READY, GET SET!

What child wouldn't be excited to touch a moon rock, see Dorothy's ruby slippers, or cruise along the C&O Canal in a canal boat pulled by mules? Washington may seem like a place that's mainly for grown-ups and school trips. After all, running the government of a superpower is serious stuff. But the city of the White House and the Capitol is also home to the International Spy Museum, the National Museum of Natural History, and the National Zoo. History that seems dry and dusty in the classroom comes alive for children as they visit landmarks they've seen in movies and on TV, ride horses through the same park where presidents have ridden, and watch thousands of dollars roll off the presses at the Bureau of Engraving and Printing. A big plus in Washington is that most attractions are free.

GET PREPARED
You could just take the Metro to the Smithsonian stop, get off at the National Mall, and wander around. And you'd probably have fun.

Or you can prepare yourself and your children. Flip through this book. The first time, flip through fast, and check out Abe Lincoln and his admirers in the lower right corner. Next, take the time to read the listings, and use the directories in the back of the book to find just what you're looking for. Last but not least, bring this book with you as you explore. It'll help you get even more out of your visits.

Before you leave, call for information—especially if you go on a holiday (when Washington is generally very crowded). The hours listed in this book are the usual operating hours. Some places are open longer or shorter or not at all on holidays, and fees and hours are always subject to change. For those sights that do charge admission, we list only the regular adult, student (with ID), and kids' prices; children under the ages specified are free. In addition, some discounts are offered for families or for a particular status or affiliation; it never hurts to ask.

To find current kids' activities and events going on in and around the city, look in or click on the "Weekend" section of Friday's *Washington Post* and in *Washington Parent*, a monthly publication available free at libraries and many grocery stores.

GET AROUND

For train lovers, riding Washington's Metro (subway) system can be as thrilling as exploring your destination. But before you go, remember that getting into a public restroom at Metro stations requires a special request. Buy your ticket at the Farecard machines, or better yet, let your kids put their math minds to work and put the money in the machines. The base fare is $1.35; the actual price you pay depends on the time of day and distance traveled. Children 4 and under ride free. But after you go through the turnstiles to enter, consider collecting your kids' cards. You'll need them again to exit.

Each line of the Metrorail is color coded: red, orange, blue, green, and yellow. You can move from one line to another at transfer stations. As a precaution, be sure shoelaces are tied and scarves are tucked in before you ride Metro escalators, some of which are more than 200 feet long. If your children are afraid of heights or you have a little one in a stroller, take the elevators. All the stations have them, though about a third of them are across the street from Metro entrances.

If, on the other hand, you decide to navigate behind the wheel, it's relatively easy to get your bearings in this diamond-shaped city. With the Capitol as its hub, Washington is composed of four quadrants—Northwest (NW), Northeast (NE), Southwest (SW), and Southeast (SE)—divided by North, South, and East Capitol streets and, on the west side of the Capitol, by the National Mall instead of a street. Within each of these quadrants, the roads running north and south are numbered, and east to west roads are named after letters of the alphabet. (You won't find an A or B street because A Street became the Mall and East Capitol Street and B Street was renamed Constitution Avenue to the north and Independence Avenue to the south.) After the lettered streets come longer street names in alphabetical order, and the alphabetical lineup repeats itself until the Maryland and Virginia borders. Add to the mix a number of diagonal avenues named for states, the most prominent being Massachusetts, Connecticut, and Pennsylvania avenues. Traffic circles and one-way streets can add to the confusion for adults but can be fun for kids, who can look for the statues and fountains in the centers of the circles.

Around the outskirts, the Capital beltway girds Washington like—you guessed it—a big belt. If you do go downtown, keep in mind that parking may be limited and expensive, especially during the week. For most suburban sights, parking is free and plentiful.

GET ORIENTED

When you arrive at a sight, be prepared to walk through metal detectors and open your bags for security personnel. Visit the information desk for maps and brochures, and inquire about children's programs. Also, show your kids how to recognize staff or security people, and designate a time and place—some visible landmark—to meet in case you become separated. It goes without saying that you should keep an eye on your children at all times, especially if they are small.

GET GOING

Finally, after you've planned and scheduled and traveled, have fun. And try to be as spontaneous as your children.

GET IN TOUCH

We'd love to hear from you. What did you and your children think about the places we recommend? Have you found other places we should include? Send us your ideas via email (c/o editors@fodors.com, specifying *Around Washington, D.C. with Kids* on the subject line) or snail mail (c/o Around Washington, D.C. with Kids, Fodor's Travel, 1745 Broadway, New York, NY 10019). In the meantime, get ready, get set, and go have a great time seeing Washington, D.C. with your kids!

—Kathryn McKay

ARLINGTON NATIONAL CEMETERY

A cemetery doesn't seem like a place for children, but this one, the most famous and most visited cemetery in the country, is different. Even the most cynical observer of Washington politics may find a lump in his throat or a tear in his eye while here, on top of which there's plenty here to see.

At the Tomb of the Unknowns, the resting place for unidentified fallen soldiers, soldiers from the Army's 3rd U.S. Infantry Regiment (Old Guard) keep watch 24/7, regardless of weather. Each sentinel marches 21 steps (children can count them silently), clicks his or her heels, and faces the tomb for 21 seconds, symbolizing the 21-gun salute—all while carrying an M-14 rifle weighing 10 pounds. The changing of the guard is a precise ceremony, held every half hour during the day from April through September and every hour the rest of the year. (At night, when the cemetery's closed, it's every two hours.)

Kids may also be interested in famous gravesites. More than 300,000 American war dead and many notable Americans are interred in these 624 acres. Even kids who don't yet know

MAKE THE MOST OF YOUR TIME You can reach Arlington on the Metro, by foot over Arlington Memorial Bridge (southwest of the Lincoln Memorial), or by car—there's a large parking lot by the visitor center on Memorial Drive. Also, the Tour-mobile bus (www.tourmobile.com, tel. 202/554–7950) and Old Town Trolley (www.old-towntrolley.com, tel. 202/832–9800) both have Arlington National Cemetery stops in their loops.

 West end of Memorial Bridge, Arlington, VA.
Metro: Arlington National Cemetery

 703/607–8000;
www.arlingtoncemetery.org

 Free; parking $1.75 for
first hr; $3.50 per hr
thereafter. Tourmobile
$7.50, children 3–11
$3.75

 Apr–Sept, daily 8–7;
Oct–Mar, daily 8–5

 6 and up

the name John F. Kennedy may find the eternal flame at his final resting place fascinating. He's buried near two of his children, who died in infancy, and his wife, Jacqueline Bouvier Kennedy Onassis. His is the most visited grave in the country. If the flame is extinguished by rain, wind, or any other cause, a continuously flashing electric spark reignites it. Nearby, a simple white cross marks the resting place of his brother Robert. Although William Howard Taft, 27th president and Supreme Court justice, lies here, as do famous veterans Joe Louis (boxer), and Abner Doubleday (reputed inventor of baseball), the sobering sea of marble tombstones in Section 60 may have the most present-day resonance: This is where more than 600 men and women who died in Iraq and Afghanistan are buried.

If you like this sight, you may also like the Washington National Cathedral (#5).

KEEP IN MIND
Kids might think the Old Guard soldiers look cool in their sunglasses, but the soldiers are not making a fashion statement—they're protecting their eyes from the sun's glare off the white marble of the tomb.

EATS FOR KIDS Plan carefully. No food or drink is allowed at the cemetery, but you can purchase and drink bottled water at the **Women in Military Service for America Memorial** near the entrance.

AUDUBON NATURALIST
SOCIETY'S WOODEND

Don't let bad weather keep the kids inside. In fact, no matter what it's like outside, there'll be something interesting to see and do at this nature wonderland. Snow and mud make finding animal tracks easier as you play nature detective. On hot, humid days, crickets and cicadas form a chorus and butterflies dance in wildflower meadows. On cool, crisp fall days, you can see varied leaf colors reflected in the large pond. But on any day, you'll hear the trill of birdsong, because the Audubon Naturalist Society (ANS) has turned the grounds into a nature preserve.

A self-guided nature trail winds through this verdant 40 acres and around the local ANS's suburban Maryland headquarters. The estate is known as Woodend, as is the mansion, which was designed in the 1920s by Jefferson Memorial architect John Russell Pope. Allowing time to marvel at Mother Nature, you can complete the ¾-mi trail in about one hour. Parents of babies should use a carrier rather than a stroller, as most of the trail has wood chips. Along the nature trail, you'll see not only birdhouses and bird feeders, but also houses for flying squirrels.

KEEP IN MIND The beauty and peace of this sanctuary might be punctured from time to time by the sight of a Cooper's hawk making a meal out of a mourning dove, the remains of a mouse that an owl discarded, or by the roar of the Washington Beltway.

EATS FOR KIDS You can pack a picnic for your Woodend adventure at nearby **Chevy Chase Supermarket** (8531 Connecticut Ave., tel. 301/656–5133), a neighborhood institution since 1958. Or about 3 mi west, in downtown Bethesda, you can nibble your way around the world at any of 180 restaurants. As its name implies **Mama Lucia's** (4907 Cordell Ave., tel. 301/907–3399) specializes in Italian dishes. Monday is pasta special night; on Tuesday, pizza prices are slashed. Friendly, quick service and red chili-pepper lights swooping across the ceiling make **California Tortilla** (4862 Cordell Ave., tel. 301/654–8226) a favorite for families. For a dining guide call the Bethesda Urban Partnership at 301/215–6660.

 8940 Jones Mill Rd., Chevy Chase, MD

 301/652-9188;
www.audubonnaturalist.org

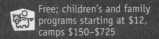 Free; children's and family
programs starting at $12,
camps $150–$725

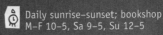 Daily sunrise–sunset; bookshop
M–F 10–5, Sa 9–5, Su 12–5

 3–9 (camps for teens, too)

For a break from the outdoors (but not the heat—the mansion isn't air-conditioned), ask at the Woodend office if you can see the old library. Along with books for adults, it contains hundreds of stuffed American birds. The mansion is rented for weddings, bar mitzvahs, and other celebrations, but it's generally open on weekdays 9–5.

During family programs (which include parents), classes, and one- to two-week camps, educated naturalists foster environmental awareness and unlock nature's mysteries. Each program focuses on a nature-oriented theme, such as flying squirrels, meadow habitats, pond life, or "metamorphosis magic," and includes such hands-on activities as catching insects, fishing for pond creatures with nets, or investigating rotting log communities. The ANS annual fair on the first Sunday in May attract thousands. While you shop at the crafts and green fair, your children can enjoy animal demonstrations.

If you like this sight, you may also like Rock Creek Park (#19).

MAKE THE MOST OF YOUR TIME Wear old
clothes and apply your sunscreen and bug repellent before you arrive. If you're with a little one and want to be able to use your stroller, head down the driveway from the parking lot. When you reach the huge walnut tree, you're near what some kids call the "secret pond." Every stick, leaf, rock, and insect needs to stay at Woodend. If your little collectors are disappointed by this rule, you can visit the bookshop. It sells souvenirs for young naturalists, including nature books, puzzles, T-shirts, and games.

BOWIE BAYSOX BASEBALL

Minor-league baseball offers major-league fun for young fans of the Bowie Baysox, a Class AA Eastern League affiliate of the Baltimore Orioles. Not only can you see what's happening better at the 10,000-seat Prince George's Stadium than at 50,000-seat, major-league ballparks, but you'll find as much action off the field as there is on it.

As a Baysox player slides into base, your children can jump around on a moon bounce at their own play area on the concourse area in view of the first base line. As players circle the diamond, your kids can circle on a carousel, which runs during the entire game, except while the national anthem plays. Little hurlers test their throwing arms in pitch-speed games.

Meanwhile, young collectors can spread out their baseball card collections in the ample bleachers, and there's plenty of room for teenagers to move a few seats away and pretend they're not really with Mom or Dad. When the ballpark is crowded, fans get more boisterous, which is also part of the entertainment. Giveaways and games throughout the summer can

MAKE THE MOST OF YOUR TIME Two Class A minor-league teams also play in Washington's outfield: the **Frederick Keys** (tel. 877/846–5397; www.frederickkeys.com) in Frederick County, Maryland, and the **Potomac Nationals** (tel. 703/590–2311; www.potomacnationals.com) in Prince William County, Virginia. The Bowie stadium is a little larger, and since the Baysox are Class AA, the quality of play is a little better. Otherwise the experience is similar. Based on where you live or where you're visiting, you may want to try one of the others.

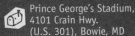 Prince George's Stadium,
4101 Crain Hwy.
(U.S. 301), Bowie, MD

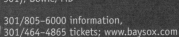 301/805-6000 information,
301/464-4865 tickets; www.baysox.com

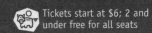 Tickets start at $6; 2 and
under free for all seats

 Early Apr–Labor Day

 4 and up

yield such precious kid keepsakes as bobble heads. Hugs from characters such as Clifford, WordGirl, and Alpha Pig happen during every game. On Saturday nights, holidays, and occasional weeknights, postgame fireworks light up the sky.

Of course, if your kids are actually interested in the game itself, they can keep track of it on electronic scoreboards and a large screen that shows replays from the field and fans in the stands. (So smile! You may be on camera.) And if your kids come wearing their youth athletic uniforms, they'll get in free Sunday through Thursday. All the activity makes minor-league baseball and children a natural double-play combination. The only real downside is that your family won't see today's superstar . . . but you might see tomorrow's!

If you like this sight, you may also enjoy the Washington Nationals (#4).

KEEP IN MIND
For diehard fans, it's easier to get autographs here than at major-league stadiums. Baysox officials recommend arriving an hour before the game to catch players between warm-ups and game time. Several players move up to the majors each year, so you never know whose signature may end up being a treasure later.

EATS FOR KIDS At the **Kids' Stand,** peanut-butter sandwiches, juice, and such typical baseball fare as hot dogs cost $1 each. (Sorry, the Kids' Stand is just for kids!) Adults pay a little more at the concession stands but get more choices. You can eat pub-type fare while watching the game from the **Diamond View** restaurant, when it's open. On most weekends and some weekdays it's booked for parties.

BUREAU OF ENGRAVING AND PRINTING

65

Show me the money! It's here—some $907 million printed daily—and we defy you not to enjoy watching as bills roll off the presses. And despite the lack of free samples, the guided, 35-minute bureau tour is one of the city's most popular attractions.

The United States began printing paper currency in 1862 to finance the Civil War and because there was a coin shortage. Two men and four women separated and sealed by hand $1 and $2 U.S. notes printed by private companies. Today, the bureau employs approximately 2,500 people, who work out of two buildings: this one and one in Fort Worth, Texas.

On tour, your children can look through wide windows to see how money really gets made. First, color is added to the paper. Then, both sides of the bills are printed in large 32- or 50-note sheets. The older machines print back side first. Newer machines print front and back simultaneously. (Bureau employees refer to bills as "notes.") Third, machines inspect the notes for defects. For example, if a sheet was folded instead of flat during

EATS FOR KIDS There's something for everyone at the **U.S. Department of Agriculture Cafeteria** (12th and C Sts. SW, tel. 202/488–7279). Show your ID and get visitor stickers at the front desk, then choose from seven food stations and a buffet. Choices include grilled cheese and hot hearty meals with veggies.

MAKE THE MOST OF YOUR TIME March–August, required same-day timed-entry tickets are issued starting at 8 at the Raoul Wallenberg Place SW ticket booth. Waits to get in can be up to two hours, and if a tour bus arrives as you do, you may be stuck outside longer. September–February is considered an off-peak time, so tickets are not required and waits likely will not be as long. While waiting, examine some money with your kids and amuse them with some fun facts. For example: If you spent $1 every second, it would take 317 years to spend $10 billion; a mile-high stack of currency would contain over 14½ million notes.

14th and C Sts. SW. Metro: Smithsonian
(Independence Ave. exit)

 Free

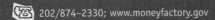 202/874-2330; www.moneyfactory.gov

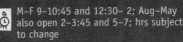 M–F 9–10:45 and 12:30– 2; Aug–May
also open 2–3:45 and 5–7; hrs subject
to change

 5 and up

the process, the notes may only be half printed. Rejects are shredded and sold or recycled. In the final area, serial numbers and Federal Reserve seals are printed, and the notes are cut.

Each $1 note costs 4¢–5.2¢ to print. Each $100 note costs about 13¢ because of security enhancements such as watermarks, color-shifting ink, and security threads. Hold one of these bills up to the light to see the vertically embedded threads. Environmentally minded kids will be glad to learn that no trees are cut down to make paper currency; it's made of 75% cotton and 25% linen.

It may sound crazy to adults, but kids like to buy bags of shredded money in the bureau's gift shop. A small bag costing a few dollars contains $150 worth of bills that didn't pass inspection. For about $5 your children can get slightly more practical mementos: postcards that look like currency with their photos on them.

If you like this sight, you may also like the National Gallery of Art (#34), where you can see paintings of some of the men on the money.

KEEP IN MIND Would you like to make money? Ten-year-old Emma Brown did. She was the youngest employee in bureau history, but she didn't work here for the fun of it. Emma's brother, the family breadwinner, was killed in action during the Civil War, leaving Emma to care for her disabled mother and the rest of the family. Emma's congressman gave her a political appointment so she could make money by making money.

C&O CANAL NATIONAL
HISTORICAL PARK'S BOAT RIDES

64

When you hear the horn blow, boarding time is near. Your family can take a leisurely, mule-drawn boat ride through the lock, down the Chesapeake & Ohio (C&O) Canal, and back again. Although you won't go far physically—less than a mile—you can mentally travel all the way back to the 1800s as costumed guides teach you about canal life. Interestingly, the C&O goes to neither the Chesapeake nor the Ohio. The Baltimore & Ohio (B&O) Railroad beat the canal to the Ohio River, and the railroad's success eventually put the canal out of business. Ironically, construction of both the C&O and the B&O began on the same day, July 4, 1828. When canal construction ended in 1850, there were 74 lift locks stretching from downtown D.C. to Cumberland, Maryland. Nevertheless, for a time the canal did prove to be economical for traders moving goods, especially coal, to the port of Georgetown, from which ships traveled to the lower Chesapeake and the Atlantic Ocean.

Most children are fascinated by the canal boat's engines: four mules named Ada, Molly, Lil, and Nell take turns pulling the 12-foot-wide barge along the towpath. As the boat passes

MAKE THE MOST OF YOUR TIME Across M Street is the oldest building in Washington: the **Old Stone House** (3051 M St. NW, tel. 202/426–6851), built in 1764. Rooms are furnished with simple, sturdy artifacts of 18th-century life, but usually the best part for kids is the garden in back. Admission is free.

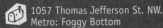 1057 Thomas Jefferson St. NW.
Metro: Foggy Bottom

 202/653–5190;
www.nps.gov/choh

 $5 ages 4 and up;
children 3 and under
ride free

 Early Apr–late Oct, W–Su 11, 1:30,
and 3 (times may change; call ahead)

 4 and up

under the 15-foot-wide bridge at Thomas Jefferson Street, it may only be a canal worker's foot keeping the boat from hitting the bridge.

Amid tales of canal life, the guides may treat you to some music and a few jokes. One example: "Along the canal, you may notice moss on the sides of the lock. Can you guess the name of the bird that uses the moss for its nest? The lock moss nester!" The rest of the ride should be all downhill.

If you like this sight, you may also like Great Falls (#50). You'll get another look at the canal and another chance to see the mules.

KEEP IN MIND
Don't be alarmed if your guide jumps off the boat to help with the lines and puts a child in charge for a few minutes. Said child will probably take possession of the horn and may even wear a captain's hat to make sure passengers stay in line. Eventually the guide will come back and your little captain will go back to being a kid.

EATS FOR KIDS Drop anchor at **Georgetown Park** (3222 M St. NW, tel. 202/342–8190), an upscale shopping mall with a basic food court. If you'd like a view of the Potomac and can pluck down a 20 spot for lunch, consider **Tony and Joe's** (tel. 202/944–4545), where you can watch seagulls looking for their own food.

THE CASTLE (SMITHSONIAN BUILDING)

63

I n London, castles may be for kings and queens, but here in Washington, the Castle is for us common folk who want to map out a day on the National Mall, a historic expanse of lawn between the Potomac River and Capitol Reflecting Pool. Called the Castle because of its magnificent towers and turrets, this first Smithsonian building is a Norman-Medieval-Revival style structure made of red sandstone. Completed in 1855, it originally housed all of the Smithsonian's operations—hard to imagine now—including the science and art collections and research laboratories. It was even the home of the first secretary of the Smithsonian and his family.

In the 1890s American buffalo (aka bison) were kept in a pen behind the Castle. These once-numerous beasts had been hunted so relentlessly for decades that their numbers were dwindling. Determined to prevent their extinction, Samuel Pierpont Langley, the Smithsonian's third secretary, convinced Congress to provide a site where bison and other animals could be protected and displayed. This decision marked the beginning of the National Zoo.

MAKE THE MOST OF YOUR TIME Since the Castle opens an hour and a half before the other Mall museums, early risers can get a good jump on their adventures.

EATS FOR KIDS The following Smithsonian museums on the Mall have food courts (*see* each listing): the National Air and Space Museum, National Museum of American History, National Museum of the American Indian, and the National Museum of Natural History. But maybe what you really require to get going is a morning pastry and coffee or an afternoon ice cream in the Smithsonian's Castle.

1000 Jefferson Dr. SW. Metro: Smithsonian

 Free

 Daily 8:30–5:30

 202/633–1000, 202/357–1729 TTY; www.si.edu

 2 and up

Start at the Castle's Smithsonian Information Center, where you can learn all about the museum, education, and research complex—19 museums and galleries (10 of which are on the National Mall) and a zoo—that is the Washington area's Smithsonian Institution and the largest museum complex in the world. An 18-minute video overview plays constantly—if your kids will sit still that long, you may get to watch it. Better yet, talk to the very knowledgeable volunteers, or pick up a brochure. Touch-screen monitors at heights for both children and adults display information on visitor services. Interactive videos provide more detailed information on the museums as well as other attractions in the capital city. Push a button on the electronic map to locate Arlington National Cemetery or to light up the entire Metro system. There's also a scale model of the National Mall and a Braille map of the city wasn't designed for children, but draws them nonetheless.

If you like this sight, you may also like to know that the monuments on the Mall are open in the morning for early birds.

KEEP IN MIND You can't see the Smithsonian's entire collection of objects, artifacts, specimens, and creatures—137 million and growing, due to gifts, purchases, and, at the zoo, births—as only an estimated 1%–2% of the collections are on display, but unlike the stuff under kids' beds, objects are cataloged and used in research. If you're short on time, stop by the Commons to view America's Treasure Chest that provides a sampling of objects from each museum.

CHILDREN'S MUSEUM OF ROSE HILL
MANOR PARK

The first place kids go in this historic home is the same one they seek out in most houses: the playroom. However, the playroom of this Georgian home, the last residence of the first elected governor of Maryland, is full of replicas of toys and games from more than 100 years ago: corncob checkers, a dollhouse, a rocking horse, a tea set, dress-up clothes, and mechanical coin banks.

Costumed guides meet families in the playroom, and the antique adventure continues. Upstairs there's a master bedroom, domestic quarters, a study room, and a child's bedroom. A 1½-hour tour at most historical sights would be too long for kids, but guides here are experienced in showing children what life was like during our country's infancy. Along the way, they explain how fireplaces, bed warmers, and windows were used in different weather and how people lived without modern conveniences. In addition, the tour includes numerous hands-on activities. Back downstairs, children can card wool, operate a loom, add stitches to a quilt, or try out 19th-century cooking equipment. If the tour gets tiresome for your kids, you can escape to the gardens, where there's room to romp.

MAKE THE MOST OF YOUR TIME Rose Hill Manor is well worth the 50-mi drive from D.C. Take Interstate 270 north to U.S. 15 at Frederick, exiting at Motter Avenue. Turn left on 14th Street and left on North Market Street. The entrance is just past the Governor Thomas Johnson High School.

 1611 N. Market St. (Rte. 355), Frederick, MD

 301/694-1650;
www.rosehillmuseum.com

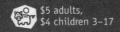 $5 adults,
$4 children 3-17

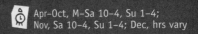 Apr-Oct, M-Sa 10-4, Su 1-4;
Nov, Sa 10-4, Su 1-4; Dec, hrs vary

 5-12

The tour itself continues outside to a one-room log cabin, a reminder that the majority of people in the early 1800s were not to the manor born. Most settlers lived in simple homesteads. In the blacksmith's shop, kids learn how 19th-century "smithies" spent most of their time repairing such ironwork as axes and chains. In the carriage museum, your children can find foot warmers in carriages and sleighs but they can't climb onto the exhibits. They can play in the Early American garden and orchard that contains more than 100 species of herbs, flowers, fruits, and vegetables. If you're interested, the last tour stop is the requisite museum store, which carries postcards and inexpensive trinkets.

If you like this sight, you may also like the Sully Historic Site (#14). They're both old houses with big backyards conducive to games of tag.

KEEP IN MIND
During the Civil War Encampment in July, Union and Confederate soldiers march, fire cannons, and talk to kids about life in the 1800s. If military history isn't for you, consider the ice-cream festival in August.

EATS FOR KIDS You can pack your own lunch or purchase some crackers or candy in the museum store and spread out at picnic tables anytime. **Pretzel and Pizza Creations** (210 N. Market St., tel. 301/694-9299) puts a new twist on pretzels, whose 30 varieties include chocolate, peanut butter, and rainbow sprinkle. Children's books on shelves in the back and cups of cappuccino encourage kids and their parents to linger.

CLAUDE MOORE COLONIAL FARM

61

ack in the 1770s, children didn't have to go to school, wear shoes, or take a nightly bath. Some modern children might even think those early days were easy—that is, until they visit this re-created Colonial farm. Here child volunteers portraying Colonial kids (when school is closed) explain that children couldn't go to school because they worked all day on the farm. Those who could fit into one of the few pairs of shoes a family might own were lucky, as they were less likely to suffer from sore feet. Frequent baths weren't considered healthful—nor were they practical, since heating enough water for a tub took a long time.

Even when the Colonial kids aren't here, you and your children can watch a pair of historical interpreters, dressed in period clothing, demonstrate how a farming couple eked out a living by tending to tobacco and wheat fields, a vegetable garden, farm animals, and family chores.

MAKE THE MOST OF YOUR TIME Encourage your kids to go to the bathroom before you arrive. The farm is equipped with the modern-day equivalent of outhouses (the portable toilet).

EATS FOR KIDS If you packed a lunch, grab one of the picnic tables at the farm entrance. A few miles away, the **McLean Family Restaurant** (1321 Chain Bridge Rd., tel. 703/356–9883) has been serving Greek and American dishes for more than 35 years. At **Rocco's Italian Restaurant** (1357 Chain Bridge Rd., tel. 703/821–3736), child-size pizzas are best sellers, but those with more sophisticated palates can order manicotti, rigatoni, and ravioli. After eating, kids (and adults) can get a lollipop for the road.

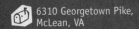 6310 Georgetown Pike,
McLean, VA

 703/442-7557;
www.1771.org

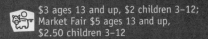 $3 ages 13 and up, $2 children 3–12;
Market Fair $5 ages 13 and up,
$2.50 children 3–12

 Apr–mid-Dec, W–Su 10–4:30

 2 and up

A dirt path winds around an orchard, fields, a tobacco barn, a pond, a hog pen, and an English-style one-room farmhouse. The walk is comfortable, and a well-napped preschooler can make the trip. Pushing a stroller along the root-laced path is tricky, but it is possible.

During Market Fairs, held the third full weekends in May, July, and October, families enjoy making Colonial crafts (about $1 each), marching in parades, and watching puppet shows. And just as in the 1770s, you can eat and shop. Check out the rosemary chicken and vegetables roasted over a fire, fresh-baked pies, and more. Reproductions of 18th-century pottery, jewelry, fragrant soaps, clothing, and toys are for sale on Market Fair days.

If you like this sight, you may also like the National Colonial Farm in Accokeek, Maryland, on the shore of the Potomac River directly across from Mount Vernon (www.accokeek.org).

KEEP IN MIND When Colonial kids played, they either used their imaginations or made toys out of things that had no monetary value and weren't needed elsewhere. They made marbles out of clay and turned split sapling trees into hoops, which they rolled on the ground with a stick. Try rolling a hula hoop with a stick. It's harder than you might think.

COLLEGE PARK AVIATION MUSEUM

Walk by the animatronic Wilbur Wright and he'll tell you about the thrills and chills of teaching pilots to fly in 1909. Children don't have to just take Wilbur's word for it: They'll see it for themselves at this interactive museum dedicated to early aviation.

Your children will be challenged and exhilarated as they turn and pull levers, knobs, and switches on flight simulators. They can try starting a plane's engine, not by turning a key as it's done today, but the way it was done before World War I, by turning a propeller. (Hint: Make sure no one is in the way and push down as hard as you can. Then step back. It's loud!) Your kids can even dress like pilots of yore, donning goggles, silk scarves, and helmets to pose for pictures against an airplane backdrop. Turn on the fan to set the scarf blowing in the wind.

Also inside, a full-scale replica of the 1911 Wright B Aeroplane, a restored 1918 Curtiss Jenny, a 1932-era Monocoupe, and a Berliner Helicopter grace the largest gallery of this airy museum, which opened in 1998. If you notice a similarity to the National Air and Space Museum, you're not imagining it; both museums were designed by the same

MAKE THE MOST OF YOUR TIME For a list of what's happening on the day you visit, check the flight desk at the front of the museum. It may list "How Things Fly," of interest to older kids, or Peter Pan Club activities, such as making paper airplanes, for preschoolers. In addition, when Maryland or Prince George's County public schools are closed, the museum sponsors aviation craft activities. If you don't make your own souvenir, though, you may want to take home a flight of fancy from the museum's gift shop, which is full of aviation toys and games, many under $5.

 1985 Cpl. Frank Scott Dr., College Park, MD.
Metro: College Park

 $4 adults,
$2 children 2–18
and students

 Daily 10–5

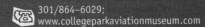 301/864–6029;
www.collegeparkaviationmuseum.com

 2 and up

architectural firm. But here you can see and do everything in an hour and you won't have to worry about losing your children in crowds.

For an extra dollar, amateur aviators can "pitch" and "roll" hand controls of the Wright Experience Flight Simulator to maneuver turns and gain altitude while flying over computerized 3-D images of historic College Park Airport as it appeared when the Wright Brothers were teaching the first military pilots to fly. Instant replay lets the pilots experience their crash or successful landing once again.

Outside there's more to see and do. Children ages 5 and under get a feel for flying by riding around in wooden planes on a mini-runway. Gaze out the museum's large glass wall onto College Park Airport, the world's oldest continually operating airport.

If you like this sight, you may also like the National Air and Space Museum (#40).

KEEP IN MIND

Since the first edition of this book came out in 2000, this museum is the number-one place that readers say they're happy to know about. Kids love it. It's best to drive, because the nearest Metro stop, College Park, is a significant walk from the museum (about 15 minutes), and because it's on the Green Line, it means a transfer for many people. Fortunately, parking is plentiful.

EATS FOR KIDS If your kids like to watch planes, bring lunch and eat on the museum balcony, overlooking the airport. You'll need to get back in the car for restaurant fare, but this college town offers lot of cheap choices. Chocolate-chip pancakes and other breakfast foods are served all day at **Plato's Diner** (7150 Baltimore Ave., tel. 301/779–7070). A plate of noodles is less than $5 at **Noodles and Company** (7320 Baltimore Ave. [Route 1], tel. 301/779–5300).

CORCORAN GALLERY OF ART

59

Create a flip book like the flip art in this book. Style your own fashion photo shoot. Turn everyday objects into works of art. These are some of the activities in store during family programs at one of the oldest U.S. museums.

During the Corcoran's Family Days, the museum becomes a family funfest. For example, a February program may involve looking for portraits of presidents. To celebrate the photography of Ansel Adams, the day may include stories of the Wild West, lasso roping demonstrations, and Native American dancing. During "DIY" or Do-It-Yourself weekends, you can follow a list of suggested activities in a guide and follow up with hands-on activities in the Education Workshop. Call for a calendar or go to the Web site and click on education.

If you can't make one of these events, you can still create a fun family adventure by sharing your enthusiasm for art with your children. The permanent collection at the Corcoran, one of the few large, private museums in Washington outside the Smithsonian family,

MAKE THE MOST OF YOUR TIME If you're up for another art gallery, the much smaller but free Renwick Gallery (8th and F Sts., tel. 202/633–7970, www. americanart.si.edu) is a few blocks away. Lots of kids like *Game Fish* by Larry Fuente, made of hundreds of little game pieces, such as dice, blocks, and darts.

EATS FOR KIDS The Corcoran Gallery's **Café des Artistes** looks too elegant for little children, but high chairs and a kids' menu let you know that even the littlest child is welcome. The Corcoran's Jazz Gospel Brunch on Sunday is festive for families. If you'd rather dine on paper plates than china, **Burrito Brothers** (1825 I St. NW, tel. 202/887–8266), a Mexican fast-food restaurant, is a few blocks away in the Ronald Reagan Building. For other casual eateries, *see* the DAR Museum and the White House.

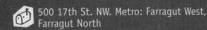
500 17th St. NW. Metro: Farragut West, Farragut North

202/639-1700;
www.corcoran.org

$10 adults, $8 students 13–18;
free children 12 and under;
July and Aug two admissions
for the price of one

W–Su 10–5, Th 10–9;
holiday Mondays 10–5

5 and up

numbers more than 14,000 works, including paintings by the first great American portraitists: John Singleton Copley, Gilbert Stuart, and Rembrandt Peale. In fact, the portrait on the $1 bill was modeled on Stuart's *Portrait of George Washington*. A replica (by the artist's own hand) is at the gallery. There's also a huge painting, *George Washington Before Yorktown*, by Rembrandt Peale. One of 17 children, 5 of whom were named for artists, Peale took some liberties with reality. Washington's horse, Nelson, was actually brown, but Peale painted him white, perhaps to stand out against the mainly brown background. (Incidentally, at times Washington did own white horses.) Ask at the front desk if these paintings of Washington are hanging that day; if they are, hand your kids dollar bills and have them try to find them.

If you like this sight, you may also like the National Museum of Women in the Arts (#26).

KEEP IN MIND I thought it would be cool to take my kids and their cousins to the Corcoran. It was, until we got to the Salon Doré, where the guards were practically stalking us. Looking back, I can't blame them. After all, it may not have been too wise of me to take three children under the age of 5 into a gilded room, even if the walls displayed sports equipment and musical instruments.

DAR MUSEUM

Move over Paul Revere or, better yet, dismount! Docents at the DAR (Daughters of the American Revolution) Museum love to share the legend of Sybil Ludington. At 16, Sybil was said to have taken off on her horse to warn folks that the British had come to Danbury, Connecticut. Legend has it that Sybil rode sidesaddle on a big bay horse for 40 mi—26 mi more than Revere—through a dangerous no-man's land between British and American lines. Whether her story is true or not, scholars don't know. The daring deeds of women were rarely documented during the days of the Revolutionary War, but a statue of Sybil is on display in the museum.

Modern kids discover what life was like 150 years or so B.C. (before computers) as part of the Colonial Adventure program (two-week advance reservation required). The journey begins with dressing the part. Boys wear vests and three-corner caps. Girls don long white aprons, because proper Colonial ladies never showed their ankles. Docents, who are all DAR members and who also wear Colonial garb, then lead the children on a special tour, describing life in Colonial America.

MAKE THE MOST OF YOUR TIME If your children have particular interests, inform your docent. Kids with an ear for music should see the antique instruments in the Rhode Island room. In wealthy homes, parents often encouraged their daughters to play a keyboard instrument and their sons to play the flute or violin.

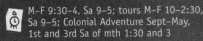

While the younger ones are visiting their own version of 18th-century America, parents and older siblings can take their own tour. Docents weave tales of women's contributions into their descriptions of the museum's 31 period rooms, named after states.

Your kids might think the Oklahoma room, set up like a Colonial kitchen, is cool. The Georgia room depicts a Savannah tavern, where citizens gathered for the state's first reading of the Declaration of Independence. In the New Hampshire room, docents describe 18th- and 19th-century dolls. And the Wisconsin room depicts a one-room house like those that only quite fortunate families could afford in Colonial times.

If you like this sight, you may also like the Children's Museum of Rose Hill Manor Park (#62).

KEEP IN MIND For some parents, one of the best parts of Colonial Adventure is getting an adult tour of the museum without having to entertain the little ones!

EATS FOR KIDS Kids might not care that Clara Barton was known as the Angel of the Battlefield and founder of the American Red Cross, but they may appreciate getting a bite to eat at the café named for her located in the American Red Cross building (1730 E St. NW), open 7–2, Monday through Friday. The lines are short, but the list of selections is long at the **Bread Line** (1751 Pennsylvania Ave. NW, tel. 202/822–8900), where you can get smoothies, sandwiches, and fresh-baked breads, bagels, and muffins on weekdays.

D.C. DUCKS

57

What do you get when you cross a tour bus with a boat? A duck, of course—that is, a D.C. Duck. Your family can tour the city by both land and water without leaving your seats aboard these unusual amphibious vehicles: standard 2½-ton GM trucks in water-tight shells with propellers and seats for 28 intrepid passengers.

During the 1½-hour ride, a wise-quacking captain entertains with anecdotes and historical trivia about Washington's memorials, monuments, and historic buildings. The captain may even quiz kids about sights along the way. Answer correctly and ding—the bell rings! For example, the captain may ask what boats are represented by the three flags near the statue of Christopher Columbus in front of Union Station. No, the answer isn't the *Love Boat,* the S.S. *Minnow,* and the *Titanic,* but rather the *Niña,* the *Pinta,* and *the Santa María.* But the part of the tour that quacks kids up the most is quacking themselves—both at tourists in town and real ducks on the water.

KEEP IN MIND The United States Coast Guard requires that the DUCKS devote one seat per passenger regardless of age, so everyone on board must have a ticket.

MAKE THE MOST OF YOUR TIME If your family is more into bikes than boats or if you'd just like to tour the city a different way, consider a **Bike and Roll tour** (1100 Pennsylvania Ave. or 50 Massachusetts Ave., tel. 202/842–2453; www. bikeandroll.com). For $40 per adult, $30 for kids 12 and under (including use of a bike), you can take a 3-hour tour covering approximately 8 mi and 55 sights. Along the way, a guide discusses history, lore, and even scandals of the capital city. The trip is appropriate for ages 7 and older, and reservations are recommended.

 Union Station main entrance,
Massachusetts Ave. NE near
N. Capitol St. Metro: Union Station

 $35 ages 12 and up,
$33 under 12

 Apr–Oct, daily 10–5 (occasionally later);
M–F departures hourly, Sa–Su every ½ hr
(tickets available beginning at 9 AM)

 202/966–3825;
www.dcducks.com

4 and up

Ducks, known as DUKWs in World War II, were created to transport soldiers and supplies from ships to areas without ports. During the war more than 21,000 DUKWs were produced, mostly by women. After the war, the Army left many DUKWs abroad, and they can still be found around the world.

Starting along the city streets, the Duck keeps pace with traffic. Eventually it moves into the Potomac river, from which your children can glimpse the Pentagon, the Anacostia Helicopter Station (home of the presidential helicopters), and the War College, formerly Fort McNair, where the conspirators who plotted to kill Lincoln were tried, convicted, and hanged. Often children are invited to take the captain's seat and steer the Duck.

If you like this ride, you may also like riding the ostrich on the historic carousel at Glen Echo (#52).

EATS FOR KIDS Duck into Union Station, a bustling train station where inaugural balls have been held. More than 35 vendors offer fast food from around the world. If you prefer a restaurant, try **America** (tel. 202/682–9555), whose menu of regional foods lives up to the expansive name. Kid-pleasing offerings include peanut butter with marshmallow cream sandwiches. In November and December, request gallery seating for a bird's-eye view of the station's Holiday train exhibit.

DISCOVERY THEATER

In the midst of the mammoth museums on the Mall is a small theater that brings both our national heritage and other cultures to life. Here kids can delight in entertaining and educational performances, such as the antics of Robert Strong as he juggles bowling balls, bananas, and rakes. On a more serious note, history opens up as kids watch plays such as *How Old is a Hero,* about Ruby Bridges and other children of the Civil Rights movement. From popular tales to well-told, lesser-known tales from around the world, the Smithsonian's Discovery Theater lives up to its name.

In the S. Dillon Ripley Center west of the Castle (*see* #63), Discovery Theater is the scene of plays, puppet shows, and storytelling. Young audiences are often encouraged to take part by singing, clapping, or helping to develop characters and plots. And since you're never more than 10 rows away from the action at Discovery Theater, which seats up to 200 people, close encounters between the audience and actors are easy.

MAKE THE MOST OF YOUR TIME The "Weekend" section of the *Washington Post* lists Discovery Theater performances as well as other kid-oriented shows around town. Whichever show you select, reservations are recommended as shows often sell out and walk up tickets are not guaranteed. Plan to arrive 15 minutes early. If you're attending a 10 AM show, go around to the west entrance in the Enid A. Haupt garden, where the doors open early for Discovery Theater patrons only. Otherwise, the building itself doesn't open until 10.

S. Dillon Ripley Center,
1100 Jefferson Dr. SW.
Metro: Smithsonian

202/633-8700;
www.DiscoveryTheater.org

$5 ages 3 and up,
$6 18 and up

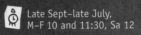

Late Sept–late July,
M–F 10 and 11:30, Sa 12

2½–14 (depending on
performance)

Though most performances are geared to preschoolers through sixth graders, some are for older children and teens. Many of these performances are held in the 550-seat Baird Auditorium at the Museum of Natural History. Performances for older kids tend to be about historical figures or events. Past examples have included *Angel in the Battlefield,* a play about Clara Barton; and *Come Sign with Me,* by Fred Beam, a performer who is deaf. Often productions are tied in with local schools' curricula.

Throughout the year, Discovery Theater celebrates cultural heritage. For example, in late September and October, Hispanic Heritage takes center stage; and in November, tales from Native Americans are highlighted. The most popular month for performances is February, when Black History Month is celebrated with songs, stories, and plays.

If you like this sight, you may also like the plays and puppet shows at Glen Echo (#52).

EATS FOR KIDS For a hot pretzel or an ice cream, check out the street vendors in front of the building. For a complete meal, walk over to the National Air and Space Museum's restaurants about 5 minutes away. Across the Mall, both the National Museum of Natural History and the National Museum of American History have restaurants (*see #27 and #30*).

KEEP IN MIND
Ride a painted pony—with stripes, polka dots, even clown faces on their saddles—on a carousel in front of the building. The lone dragon is the most desired mount and sometimes kids will let others ahead of them so they're first in line for the dragon on the next cycle.

FORD'S THEATRE
NATIONAL HISTORIC SITE

The events of April 14, 1865, which shocked the nation and closed this theater, continue to fascinate both young and old. On that night, during a performance of *Our American Cousin*, John Wilkes Booth entered the state box on the balcony and assassinated Abraham Lincoln. The stricken president was carried across the street to the house of tailor William Peterson, where he died the next morning.

After reopening following renovations in 2009, tickets are required (but free) to tour this site. Allow about an hour to hear a National Park Service ranger's interpretation of the night Lincoln was shot, go through the Lincoln Museum (in the lower level), and to cross the street to Peterson House to see the bedroom where Lincoln died. On slow days, park rangers will take visitors close to the Presidential box where Lincoln was assassinated.

In the museum, there are plenty of artifacts about the traumatic events, but the Derringer pistol that Booth used and the ornate, horn-handled dagger Booth used to stab and

MAKE THE MOST OF YOUR TIME Every year from Thanksgiving through New Year's, the ghosts of Christmases past, present, and future come to the Ford's Theatre stage in Charles Dickens's classic tale *A Christmas Carol*. (The rest of the year, performances tend to be serious adult plays.) Call 202/347–4833 for information.

EATS FOR KIDS Older kids love the **Hard Rock Cafe** (999 E St. NW, tel. 202/737–7625), which mixes rock memorabilia and tunes. For live tunes at lunchtime and lots of hot sandwiches, check out **Potbelly** (555 12th St., tel. 202/347–7100). The "Wreck" is loaded with a variety of meat. The "Big Jack," may sound intimidating but it's actually a classic PB&J. For kids who haven't graduated from the Wiggles to rock and roll or if there's a long wait, the food court at the **Old Post Office Pavilion** (1100 Pennsylvania Ave. NW, tel. 202/289–4224) may be better.

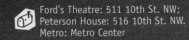
Ford's Theatre: 511 10th St. NW;
Peterson House: 516 10th St. NW.
Metro: Metro Center

 Free

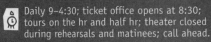
Daily 9–4:30; ticket office opens at 8:30;
tours on the hr and half hr; theater closed
during rehearsals and matinees; call ahead.

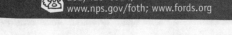 202/426–6924;
www.nps.gov/foth; www.fords.org

 7 and up

nearly kill Lincoln's theater companion, Maj. Henry R. Rathbone, seem to attract the most attention. To get your kids exploring, pick up a Junior Ranger handout, aimed at kids 6–12. Kids who complete the activities, can pick up a prize at the end.

Encourage your kids to talk to the rangers on staff. It might seem strange at first to see rangers in museum settings instead of big national parks, but since Washington, D.C., is a federal district full of national monuments and historic sites, rangers are a common sight and a great resource.

If your family likes this sight, they may also have interest in seeing the actual bullet that killed Lincoln, on display at the National Museum of Health and Medicine (#28) and the home of abolitionist Frederick Douglass (#53).

KEEP IN MIND How tall is your child? Probably not as tall as Abraham Lincoln, who was 6′4″—even more extraordinary in his day, because poor diet often stunted children's growth. Honest Abe was our tallest president. At about 5′4″, our fourth president, James Madison, was our shortest.

FRANKLIN DELANO ROOSEVELT MEMORIAL

I f you visit this memorial to our 32nd president with older children, take your time walking through its four outdoor "rooms" or galleries—each symbolic of one of Roosevelt's four terms. Waterfalls and reflecting pools are interspersed throughout and are great for dangling toes. Pause in the granite passageways between the galleries, engraved with some of Roosevelt's most famous quotes, including THE ONLY THING WE HAVE TO FEAR IS FEAR ITSELF. If you come with toddlers, however, head straight to the third room. Here, though youngsters can't sit on Roosevelt's lap, they can pet Fala, Roosevelt's Scottish terrier. The tips of Fala's ears shine from all the attention.

Assuming you come here for more than Fala, there's plenty to absorb. Challenge your children to look closely at the big bronze wall of faces in the second room; it depicts people put back to work after the Depression. See if you can find two men planting trees, an artist stirring paint, one farmer gathering oranges, and another driving a tractor. There's even a girl painting and a boy sculpting. Also in the second gallery, handprints along the columns,

EATS FOR KIDS You might find one of Roosevelt's favorite foods (hot dogs) at a food stand near the Lincoln Memorial. You might find another favorite food (fish chowder) a short drive away at **Maine Avenue Seafood Market** (1100 Maine Ave. SW), which carries fresh fish and shellfish. Maine Avenue also contains seven waterside restaurants, including local seafood powerhouse **Phillips Flagship** (900 Water St. SW, tel. 202/488–8515). All have terraces overlooking the Washington Channel and the boats moored there.

 1850 W. Basin Dr. SW, west side of
Tidal Basin. Metro: Smithsonian

 202/426-6841;
www.nps.gov/fdrm

 Free

 24 hrs; staffed daily 9:30 AM–8 PM

2 and up

representing the working hands of the American people, encourage you to touch. In the fourth room, a statue honors first lady Eleanor Roosevelt, a shy child who became a vocal spokesperson for human rights.

More than recognizing FDR's contributions, the memorial teaches children about history, war, and even disability. Due to polio, Roosevelt used a wheelchair for the last 24 years of his life, and a statue of him in a wheelchair was added to the memorial in 2001 after years of controversy. Ask an older child what's more important: that Roosevelt be seen realistically and as a role model for the disabled or that his desire not to have people see his disability be honored.

If you like this sight, you may also want to see the original monument to Roosevelt in front of the National Archives Building (#37): It was made to order. Roosevelt said if anyone put up a memorial in his honor, he would want it to be about the size of a desk.

MAKE THE MOST OF YOUR TIME

This memorial presents one of the best places for family photographs. Have your child pet Fala, take a place in the Breadline, and listen to Roosevelt's fireside chat.

KEEP IN MIND If the dog makes more of an impression on your little one than the president, many kids in the 1940s might have felt the same way. Fala was famous in his day. He sat at the feet of his master and British Prime Minister Winston Churchill when they signed the Atlantic Charter in 1941. For merchandise featuring the presidential pooch, check out the bookstore. A portion of the proceeds benefits the National Park Service.

FREDERICK DOUGLASS
NATIONAL HISTORIC SITE

Pick up tickets for the 30-minute tours in the visitor center, where a wall is devoted to this prolific speaker and writer's quotations. Among the more famous ones is, I WOULD UNITE WITH ANYBODY TO DO RIGHT AND WITH NOBODY TO DO WRONG. Here your children can shake hands with the bronze statue of Douglass, shiny gold from all the attention. The visitor center also has the Douglass family tree and a gift shop with books about Douglass.

Next you can watch the 17-minute film *Fighter for Freedom: The Frederick Douglass Story*. Douglass knew neither his mother, a slave, nor the identity of his father, a white man. At age 8, he was sent to work for a family in Baltimore, where he was exposed to the "mystery of reading" and decided that education was "the pathway to freedom." At 20 he escaped and became an abolitionist, women's rights activist, author, editor of an antislavery newspaper, minister to Haiti, and the most respected 19th-century African American orator.

KEEP IN MIND Kids may not recognize the pictures of Douglass's friends, Anthony, John Brown, Elizabeth Cady Stanton, and Harriet Tubman, but they'll probably identify the checkerboard, invalid chair, and dumbbells.

MAKE THE MOST OF YOUR TIME Though *Fighter for Freedom: The Frederick Douglass Story* is enlightening, this short film depicts a graphic beating he got when he was a slave. Some children and even adults find it disturbing, not just because of the violence but because it confronts a shameful part of our history. Encourage your kids to talk about their feelings and ask questions of you and the rangers. To enhance your children's appreciation of Cedar Hill, talk about Frederick Douglass, the Civil War, and the Civil Rights movement before you arrive.

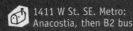

1411 W St. SE. Metro: Anacostia, then B2 bus

202/426-5961 or 202/619-7222; www.nps.gov/frdo

Free, $1.50 per person for reservations. (Groups of less than 10, call 877/444-6777; 10 or more, call 877/559-6777.)

Mid-Apr–mid-Oct, daily 9–5 tours at 9, 12:15, 1:45, 3, 3:30, and 4); mid-Oct–mid-Apr, daily 9–4 (same tour start times, but the last tour begins at 3:30)

9 and up

After the film, follow a park ranger to Cedar Hill, the first designated African American National Historic Site and the last home of Frederick Douglass.

Rangers focus on Douglass's life at Cedar Hill, first with Anna Murray, his wife of 40 years, and after her death, with second wife, Helen Pitts, who was not only 20 years his junior but also white. Douglass simply explained that his first wife was the color of his mother, his second the color of his father. Though the tour is best for children who have studied American history, rangers are skilled at engaging kids as young as kindergartners. Children learn not only about the past but also about the importance of freedom and equality, even today.

If you like this sight, you may also like another old home at Sully Historic Site (#14).

EATS FOR KIDS Unfortunately, the only place you're allowed to eat here is on the grassy hill near the visitor center, next to the parking lot, but there are no picnic tables. So you might want to eat before or after your visit.

GLEN ECHO PARK

The carousel alone would be reason enough to visit this historic park. In the center of the park, the historic Dentzel Carousel offers choices of mounts, which range from a painted pony and a majestic lion to a saber-toothed tiger and an ostrich. Like the carousel, the park offers lots of options for families.

The arts thrive here. The Adventure Theater stages such children's productions as *Go Dog Go, If You Give a Pig a Pancake,* and *Winnie the Pooh* weekends year-round in a 170-seat theater that opened in 2007. At the Puppet Co. Playhouse, nationally acclaimed puppeteers manipulate a variety of puppets in classic plays and stories in a theater that was made specifically for puppet shows. About once a week, the Playhouse hosts Tiny Tots @ 10 for wee ones up to 4 years old ($5 for all ages). *Nutcracker,* in winter, is one of the most popular productions. Reservations are recommended for this popular puppet place that seats 250.

MAKE THE MOST OF YOUR TIME Whatever event you're going to at Glen Echo, allow at least an extra 30 minutes. Just stomping over the bridge leading to the park takes time. You also may want to act out the Norwegian folktale of Billy Goats Gruff, toss stones in the creek, and take a spin around the carousel.

 7300 MacArthur Blvd.,
at Goldsboro Rd., Glen Echo, MD

 301/634-2222 (24-hr info);
301/320-1400 (visitor information);
www.glenechopark.org

 Clara Barton
National Historic
Site free; carousel
$1.25; puppet shows
$10 or plays $12-$15

 Daily 9-5; puppet shows W-F 10 and 11:30,
Sa-Su 11:30 and 1; plays Sa-Su 11 and 1:30

All ages

Nature holds its own at Glen Echo Park. A local Eagle Scout candidate established nature trails around Minnehaha Creek, near the museum. History has its place, too, and children who have studied the Civil War or women's history may enjoy a tour of the Clara Barton National Historic Site, near the park entrance. Known as the "angel of the battlefield" for nursing wounded soldiers, Clara Barton founded the American Red Cross. Rangers conduct hourly tours that give insight into her life and Glen Echo at the turn of the last century.

Finally, the park is also a great spot for recreation. When your kids need to let off steam, there's plenty of space to run around and a playground with swings, slides, and a climbing tower.

If you like this sight, you might also like the plays at Discovery Theater (#56).

KEEP IN MIND
There's more than kids' activities at this park, founded by two brothers who invented the egg beater. It's the adults who kick up their heels in the historic Spanish Ballroom. All dance events are open to the public, and most include a mini-lesson. Whether waltz, contra, salsa, or swing is your thing, you can find it here.

EATS FOR KIDS When the carousel at Glen Echo is open (May–Sept, W–Th 10–2 and Sa–Su 12–6; Sept–Oct, Sa–Su 12–6), so is the adjacent **snack bar.** But whether you bring or purchase food, you'll find enough picnic tables and wide-open spaces here to accommodate scores of families.

GODDARD SPACE FLIGHT VISITOR CENTER

Not nearly as glitzy, large, or crowded as the Smithsonian's National Air and Space Museums, this NASA-run museum, called the Visitor Center, brings space flight down to earth while letting imaginations soar. Though the center wasn't designed specifically for children, toddlers will love fiddling with the many controls that accompany the exhibits and turning on spacesuits.

The replica of the *Gemini XII* where astronauts Buzz Aldrin and Jim Lovell spent four days is as good as real for youngsters because they can go inside this compact car-size capsule and play with 100 buttons and knobs (count them!). Kids who want to look authentic can even wear spacesuits from a dress-up area.

After a trip aboard the *Gemini,* older kids may want to go on a scavenger hunt to find the speed of light (Hint: Faster than a toddler grabs a cookie), the color of young stars

KEEP IN MIND Goddard is about 9 mi from Washington, but off the beaten path. From the Baltimore–Washington Parkway (I–295) or Capital Beltway, exit to Route 193 east (Greenbelt Road). Pass the Goddard Space Flight Visitor Center, continue ¾ mi to Soil Conservation Road, and turn left. Take the next left on Explorer Road, and follow signs.

MAKE THE MOST OF YOUR TIME Show up with your elementary-school-age child for Experiment Days on the third Sunday of each month from September through June from 1 to 3. For middle-school kids, about once a month, you can even bring your own rocket (available at Goddard's gift shop), but know that you'll need about a half hour to assemble the rocket and 24 hours to let the glue dry.

Bldg. 88, Explorer Rd., Greenbelt, MD

 Free

Sept–June, T–F 10–3, Sa–Su 12–4; July–Aug, T–F 10–5, Sa 12–4; group tours by reservation only; closed on most federal holidays

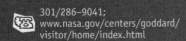 301/286–9041; www.nasa.gov/centers/goddard/ visitor/home/index.html

 2 and up, tours 9 and up

(pick from a patriotic palate), and other trivia. Winners take home a free lithographic of rockets and space shuttles, a patch commemorating the Hubble Space telescope or the James Webb telescope, or some other small flight memento.

Be sure to see Science on a Sphere. Using computers and video projectors, you can see animated movies and images of the Earth, other planets, the sun and the stars.

Outside the center is a "rocket garden," with a real 92-foot Delta rocket and other authentic space hardware. You can also see other buildings at this sprawling government complex where scientists and engineers monitor spaceships circling the Earth, the solar system, and beyond.

If you like this sight, you may also like the College Park Aviation Museum (#60).

EATS FOR KIDS Check out the display of fast food for space flight. Then to taste the real thing, purchase astronaut's freeze-dried ice-cream sandwiches in foil pouches at the gift shop. It's messy and not particularly tasty but still cool to kids. Picnicking is permitted on the grounds, but the only food sold here is soda from a vending machine. A short drive away in historic Greenbelt, the **New Deal Café** (113 Center Way, tel. 301/474–5642) gives parents a break. While waiting for your soups, sandwiches, or vegetarian—even vegan— entrées, your kids can read books, play board games, or work on puzzles.

GREAT FALLS

Thanks to the Ice Age 2 million years ago, a wide, flat, slow-moving body of water cut its way through bedrock and created Great Falls, a lovely waterfall on the Potomac adjacent to the C&O Canal National Historical Park. Here the water thrashes about faster, frothier, and noisier than the wildest bubble bath, although your kids might want to test that theory come bath time!

For information and a trail map, head to the 1831 Tavern, which still welcomes visitors, though it stopped providing food and shelter in the 1930s. Exhibits cover how a lock works, plant and animal life, and early canal life, but the main attraction at this park is the great outdoors.

If it's hiking you're after, check out these interesting options, but beware of trails too rugged for little ones. The Billy Goat Trail sounds simple, but the 4-mi loop requires scrambling over boulders. Hiking boots and athletic ability are recommended. The Gold Mine Loop also

MAKE THE MOST OF YOUR TIME You can enjoy the falls from either Maryland or Virginia (9200 Old Dominion Dr., McLean, VA, tel. 703/285–2964). The Virginia side offers more opportunities for serious rock climbers. Bring your own equipment and register at the visitor center. Swimming and wading are prohibited on both sides, but you can fish (license required for anglers 16 and older), climb rocks, or go white-water kayak-ing—experienced boaters and below the falls only, as currents are deadly. Despite signs and warnings, people occasionally dare the water, and lose.

 11710 MacArthur Blvd., Potomac, MD

301/299–3613
or 301/767–3714;
www.nps.gov/choh

 $5 vehicles, $3 per person without vehicle, good for 3 days for visiting both sides of the Falls, in MD and VA

 Park daily sunrise–sunset; tavern daily 9–4:30

 4 and up

runs a little over 3 mi, revealing the remains of an 1867–1939 mine. Not everyone went to California for gold. Sorry, panning isn't allowed today.

For a golden view of the falls that everyone enjoys, take the walkway to Olmsted Island. This 0.6-mi, wheelchair- and stroller-accessible route leads to a platform with a spectacular view of the churning waters. Along the walkway, signs alert you to ancient plants growing among the rocks. You might also see more recent arrivals: freshwater Asiatic clamshells, first reported here in the 1980s. In any case, your kids can find a cozy seat on the rocks in the middle of the platform or on the benches, and you can see Mother Nature at her wildest and woolliest.

If you like this sight, you may also like the C&O Canal (#64) in Georgetown.

KEEP IN MIND

The same mules that take visitors on a boat ride through the lock at the Chesapeake & Ohio (C&O) Canal work here, too. Rides are $7 ages 15 and up and $5 for children 4–14. The mules usually work April through October (no word on what they do the rest of the year!) but call ahead for dates and times of the rides.

EATS FOR KIDS As at all National Park Service sights, you may not feed the animals, but you can feed yourselves. Buy something at the **snack bar** (open W–Su June–July and most weekends Mar–May and Sept–Nov), a few paces north of the tavern, or bring your own picnic. Potomac Village, 3½ mi away, has two supermarkets that sell prepared foods: **Giant** (9812 Falls Rd., tel. 301/983–4246) and **Safeway** (10104 River Rd., tel. 301/983–2150). Or take off for **locally owned Potomac Pizza** (9812 Falls Rd., tel. 301/299–7900), for pizza plus calzones and sub sandwiches.

HIRSHHORN MUSEUM
AND SCULPTURE GARDEN

Any child who thinks art museums only display boring, two-dimensional paintings of old-fashioned people is in for a surprise at the Hirshhorn. Art here isn't only paint on canvas. Some art is made from mud, twigs, leaves, stone, light, video monitors, and even fat. Here a brightly colored fish mobile made of metal and glass swims. A wet dog in bronze walks. Paper flowers grow out of a wall.

American artists such as Georgia O'Keeffe, Jackson Pollock, Mark Rothko, and Frank Stella are represented along with modern European and Latin masters, including Juan Muñoz, René Magritte, and Joan Miró. Contemporary pieces by Robert Gober, Ann Hamilton, Jim Hodges, Ed Ruscha, Andy Warhol, and numerous others reflect the diversity of technique and expression of today's artists. Through acquisitions, the Hirshhorn continually adds work to the collection. Contemporary pieces by John Baldessari, Ann Hamilton, Jim Hodges, Ernesto Neto, and Lorna Simpson reflect a diversity of techniques.

KEEP IN MIND
The Hirshhorn suggests that you connect artworks with experiences meaningful to your child. Pablo Picasso's *Woman with a Baby Carriage* might elicit a story about pushing your own baby in a carriage. Although children are encouraged to get to know the art, please remind your kids that the artwork is for the eyes, not the fingers.

MAKE THE MOST OF YOUR TIME
Some of the coolest art for kids is outside in the Sculpture Garden. *Man Passing Through the Door* by Jean Ipousteguy may remind "muggles" of when Harry Potter boarded the train to Hogwarts, though instead of an owl, said man has another animal with him. Also: ask your kids to find Kenneth Snelson's tall sculpture *Needle Tower* in the plaza? Get in its center, and look up. You'll see a star.

Independence Ave. at 7th St. SW.
Metro: Smithsonian or L'Enfant Plaza,
Maryland Ave. exit

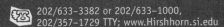
202/633-3382 or 202/633-1000,
202/357-1729 TTY; www.Hirshhorn.si.edu

 Free

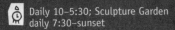
Daily 10-5:30; Sculpture Garden
daily 7:30-sunset

5 and up; Young at Art
3-12; Artlab 13-18

Okay, so most kids won't recognize or particularly care about these names. To make your museum experience fun, visit the information desk for a free "Family Guide." It's full of colorful art cards that encourage your children to search for a work, learn something about it, and relate it to their own lives and imagination. For example, on the card about Claes Oldenburg's *Geometric Mouse: Variation 1, Scale A,* kids are challenged to wonder what it would be like to be a geometric mouse visiting a mouse house with 500 other geometric mice. To design a tour for your family, allow your kids to choose their own art cards and go to the youngest child's selections first.

The Hirshhorn's ArtLab (just off the Sculpture Garden) offers classes taught by artists and art educators. Children and their parents can drop in for Gallery Tales for Tots and hands-on art projects inspired by work on view in the galleries.

If you like this sight, you may also like the sculpture garden at the National Gallery of Art (#34). Ask your kids if they can spot works by the same artists in both locations.

EATS FOR KIDS When the Hirshhorn opened in 1974, detractors who didn't like the cylindrical architecture of the museum called it the Doughnut on the Mall. On the fly food carts don't sell doughnuts, but they do carry tacos and hot dogs for carnivores and herbivores. These green-and-white carts are often in front of the Hirshhorn. But if the skies or sales are dismal, they aren't in business. For other options, check out ideas under the (Smithsonian) Castle.

INTERNATIONAL SPY MUSEUM

I spy. You spy. Everyone spies here. Whether they're eavesdropping on siblings or searching for hidden presents, kids love to spy. This museum takes the art of espionage to new levels for junior James Bonds and young Nancy Drews.

Did you know there are more spies in Washington than in any other city? Crowds of curious visitors walk through metal detectors and watch a short video on espionage before winding through the exhibits. Like little moles, kids can crawl through the museum's ductwork to peek through the vents. They find larger-than-life-size silver flies on walls that transmit information to undisclosed locations.

Despite all the cool gadgetry that makes kids want to speed too quickly in hot pursuit of adventure through the museum, take your time when you see the replica of James Bond's Aston Martin sports car. Just like in the films, gadgets galore pop out.

KEEP IN MIND For teens who want to put their sleuthing skills to work, they can crack a safe, conduct a polygraph of a suspect, weigh evidence and more through Operation Spy. This one-hour program gives participants (12 and older) a chance to "feel, think, and act" like real intelligence officers. Whether the teens succeed or fail in the mission, they get hands-on experience in the great game of espionage. Operation Spy costs an additional $10 per person (combination tickets with admission available) and reservations are not required, but recommended. The spies work in groups of about 15. Operations run about every 10 to 15 minutes. Also note: Everyone is required to exit the museum through the well-stocked gift shop.

 800 F St. NW. Metro: Gallery Place/Chinatown

 $18 adults, $15 children age 5–18, free for children under 5

 Mar, daily 9:30–6; hrs extended during the summer and holidays; closed Thanksgiving Day, Christmas, and New Year's Day

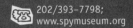 202/393–7798; www.spymuseum.org

 10 and up

Watch as people transform themselves into spies on videos that made Superman's telephone booth transition look way too simple. Through wardrobe changes, makeup, facial hair, and shoe inserts to make a person limp, a man and a woman transformed themselves into people their own close friends probably couldn't recognize.

While the museum offers clues and commentary on the capture of Robert Hanssen, Aldrich Ames, and other modern spies, a professional spy from the 12th century may draw just as much interest. In a huge glass cage, a life-size figure of a masked Ninja poses, representing the Japanese art of invisibility. Other tricks of the trade include homing pigeons with cameras, a pistol in a lipstick, and a spy kit with ropes, candles, flashlights, pliers, rubber gloves, and more.

If you like this sight, you may also like the National Air and Space Museum (#40).

EATS FOR KIDS

It's no secret that the museum's **Spy City Cafe** (tel. 202/654–0995) serves killer sandwiches, wraps, salads, and a large selection of sweets. To pursue predictable fare, cross the street to **Subway** (901 E St., tel. 202/737–3480).

MAKE THE MOST OF YOUR TIME

At peak times—spring and summer weekends, Thanksgiving, and Christmas—the museum recommends buying tickets through their Web site at least 48 hours in advance. The high-tech feel of this metallic and wood museum is particularly cool for preteens and teenagers. If you bring along a younger sibling, your child might not be only one who gets tired, as seating is limited and strollers aren't allowed in the museum (nor are food, beverages, or cameras).

KENILWORTH NATIONAL
AQUATIC GARDENS

Children like to run through this 12-acre national park devoted to aquatic plants. However, the best way to enjoy this sanctuary is to walk quietly and pause often. Hear bullfrogs croak and birds chirp, search for turtles and frogs among platter-size leaves, gaze on exotic plants and water lilies reminiscent of a Monet painting. A clever game of "I Spy" might slow the kids down enough for the park's true pleasure—bird-watching. With red-wing blackbirds, blue herons, and bald eagles there's plenty to spy.

Ask your youngsters how cattails and yellow flag irises got their names or whether pickerelweeds and rose mallow shrubs (no relation to marshmallows) look as silly as they sound. Listen to the bullfrogs and watch for turtles sunbathing and crayfish burrowing mud chimneys to escape from turtles and birds, and the beaver dams. Beavers like to dine on the water lilies, which is why the most expensive plants are close to the visitor center. Don't restrict yourselves to sight and sound: Let your other senses, like smell (tasting isn't recommended), help you explore the park, too.

MAKE THE MOST OF YOUR TIME The best time to visit is 8–11, when day-bloomers are opening and night-bloomers have yet to close. Water lilies flower through the summer.

EATS FOR KIDS Alas, there's no food for humans here (only water), and there aren't any restaurants within walking distance of these gardens tucked away in a corner of Northeast Washington. Pack a big lunch and take advantage of the picnic tables near the ponds.

 1550 Anacostia Ave. NE

 202/426-6905;
www.nps.gov/kepa

 Free

 Daily 7–4

 2 and up

If you're traveling with a toddler or preschooler, plan to spend at least 10 minutes in the visitor center, where kids can place pictures of the Gardens' animals on a mural. For groups with older kids, the center is place to pick up maps and activity booklets.

In winter, you can search for the shells of pond crustaceans left by birds and follow animal tracks. Do you think the bird got away, or did the fox eat last night? In spring, you may hunt for muskrat holes in the dikes or watch female dragonflies dip their tails in the water to lay eggs. Whatever the season, it's fun watching kids explore Kenilworth.

If you like this sight, you may also like the U.S. National Arboretum (#9).

KEEP IN MIND Driving directions are tricky; if you're using a GPS, be sure to note the zip code: 20019. If you do get lost, you should know that locals refer to Kenilworth as "lily ponds." Keep a careful eye on children, especially preschoolers, while they search for aquatic life. Although the ponds are only 3 feet deep, the banks can be slick and there are no fences around them. The only barriers are those in the ponds, designed to protect the plants. And don't worry if your clothes get a little dirty. It's all part of the fun.

THE KENNEDY CENTER

The Kennedy Center looks like a place for adults in tuxedos and black dresses, and it is. But it's also a place that rolls out the red carpet for children. As the nation's performing-arts center, it takes seriously its responsibility to make an eclectic calendar of top-notch performances accessible to many. One example is the dark-red free shuttle, which runs between the center and the Foggy Bottom Metro every 15 minutes.

More than 100 family events are held each year through the Center's Performances for Young Audiences in which actors, dancers, storytellers, musicians, and puppeteers show off for kids. The National Symphony Orchestra puts on Kinderkonzerts and family concerts. Arrive 45 minutes early before most shows and your children can beat drums, blow into a tuba, or clang cymbals. Tots and their stuffed animal friends love the popular Teddy Bear Concerts where musicians play on tiny versions of their instruments—like the ones they used when they were little.

MAKE THE MOST OF YOUR TIME Cue sheets for many children's performances are available on the Kennedy Center's Web site. Not only do the sheets provide background information on the performers and their art, but they often give kids a list of things to look for when watching a show. If you can't catch Millennium Stage performances at the center, you can see them live every evening on the center's Web site.

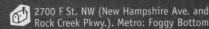 2700 F St. NW (New Hampshire Ave. and Rock Creek Pkwy.). Metro: Foggy Bottom

 Free, children's performances free–$18

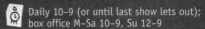 Daily 10–9 (or until last show lets out); box office M–Sa 10–9, Su 12–9

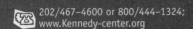 202/467–4600 or 800/444–1324; www.Kennedy-center.org

 4 and up

As part of the Performing Arts for Everyone Initiative, free one-hour performances are held nightly at 6 on the Millennium Stage (neither ticket nor reservation required). Many provide the perfect opportunity to introduce children to classical music or opera. In others, dancers, actors, storytellers, or magicians reach out to kids of all ages. Seats are generally plentiful, though kids often sit up front or on the steps, or they don't sit at all—they dance! During the September open house, at least one stage is devoted to children's performances.

Even without seeing a performance, you can enjoy this six-theater memorial to President Kennedy. Pick up a "flag sheet" at the information desk, and visit the Hall of Nations and Hall of States, where the flags of more than 140 countries and all 50 states hang, the latter in order of admission to the union.

If you like this sight, you might also like the Washington National Cathedral (#5).

KEEP IN MIND
The 618-foot-long Grand Foyer carpeted in red is a tempting place for kids to run. It's easy to understand why. The Foyer is one of the world's largest rooms. If you could lay the Washington Monument on its side in the Grand Foyer, you would still have about 3 inches to spare. Look up, and you'll see tons of crystal—literally. Each of the 18 chandeliers weighs one ton.

EATS FOR KIDS For restaurants with a view, you can't beat the top of the Kennedy Center. The **KC Café** offers self-serve soup, sandwiches, pasta salads, and pizza overlooking the Potomac and Georgetown. The formal **Roof Terrace Restaurant** isn't appropriate for most kids, but for older children with tickets to a play, it could be a great way to start the evening. Prices at both the café and the restaurant tend to be steep, but the service is quick, ensuring that you get to the show on time!

LINCOLN MEMORIAL

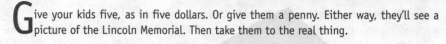

G ive your kids five, as in five dollars. Or give them a penny. Either way, they'll see a picture of the Lincoln Memorial. Then take them to the real thing.

Children eager to show off newly acquired counting skills will find plenty to keep them busy here. Thirty-six Doric columns, representing the 36 states in the country at the time of Lincoln's death, surround the somber statue of the seated Lincoln. Above the frieze are the names of the 48 states of the union when the memorial was dedicated in 1922. (Alaska and Hawaii are noted by an inscription on the terrace leading up to the memorial.)

Older children may practice their oratorical skills by reciting two of Lincoln's great speeches—the Second Inaugural Address and the Gettysburg Address—which are carved on the north and south walls. Kids can even find the exact spot (look down for the engraving added in 2003) on the steps of the Lincoln Memorial where Martin Luther King Jr. gave his famous "I Have a Dream" speech in 1963.

KEEP IN MIND If your group feels too hot after walking up the steps, check out the gift shop. It's tiny, but air-conditioned.

MAKE THE MOST OF YOUR TIME Though many visitors look only at the front and interior of the monument, there is more to explore. On the lower level, to the left of the main stairs, is Lincoln's Legacy, a display that chronicles the memorial's construction. A video and photos depict famous demonstrations and speeches that have taken place here, and another exhibit shows postage stamps from around the world that feature Lincoln on them.

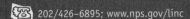

Look carefully at Lincoln's face and hands. They look especially lifelike because they were based on castings done of Lincoln while he was president. Those who know sign language might recognize that Lincoln's left hand is shaped like an A while his right hand looks like an L. Although it's a myth that this was done on purpose, Daniel Chester French, the sculptor, had a son who was deaf.

Though many visitors look only at the front and interior of the monument, there is much more to explore. On the lower level, to the left of the main stairs, is Lincoln's Legacy, a display that chronicles the memorial's construction.

If you like this sight, you might also like Ford's Theatre (#55).

EATS FOR KIDS A **refreshment stand** (French Dr., north side of Independence Ave. SW) serves sandwiches, fries, chicken fingers, just a short walk from the memorial.

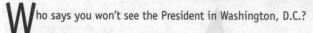

44

Who says you won't see the President in Washington, D.C.?

Here, you can get up close with all 44 of the men who have ever been POTUS (President of the United States).

Though Madame Tussauds has been entertaining Europeans with its signature wax figures for more than 200 years, this Washington, D.C., showplace just opened in 2007.

More than 100 uncannily lifelike wax figures form a virtual Who's Who of movies, music, sports, and, of course, politics featured in themed interactive exhibits. In "Sports," kids can find out how much bigger they need to grow to measure up to Babe Ruth. In the Civil Rights Room, they can take a seat next to Rosa Parks on the bus. In "Glamour," kids might not know Brad Pitt or Julia Roberts, but they'd probably like to say hello to Disney star Selena Gomez. In the "Spirit of Washington," there's a replica of the Oval Office where your

EATS FOR KIDS Enchiladas and tacos aren't the only dishes for kids at **Austin Grill** (750 E St. NW, tel. 202/393–3776); kids can order PB&J or carrots and celery sticks. **Clyde's of Gallery Place** (707 7th St. NW, tel. 202/349–3700) is part of the Clyde's restaurant group that's been serving D.C. diners for generations.

10001 F St. NW. Metro: Metro Center.

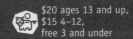 $20 ages 13 and up,
$15 4–12,
free 3 and under

 10–6

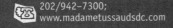 202/942-7300;
www.madametussaudsdc.com

7 and up

daughter can not only sit behind the desk, she can prop her feet up on it (if her legs are long enough!).

In "Behind the Scenes," kids can see how the wax figures are made and can compare their hands and feet of famous folk, including those of Jennifer Lopez and Evander Holyfield.

After seeing all these famous folks, your child might want to brag about it, and she can tell more than her friends: At the final stop in Madame Tussauds D.C., kids can tell all to Katie Couric, while parents and friends watch on a nearby TV monitor.

If you like this sight, you may also like the Newseum (#23), which also gives kids a chance to appear on camera.

KEEP IN MIND Your kids might wonder who Madame Tussaud was. The young Marie learned her skills from a doctor. During the French Revolution, she was captured but managed to keep her head, along with her collection of death masks of guillotined nobles. She fled to England, where these gruesome models became a touring exhibition. In addition to this attraction and the London original there are eight more Madame Tussauds in the world.

MAKE THE MOST OF YOUR TIME

You can save 15 percent off the admission if you bring your American Automobile Association (AAA) card (even though you'll probably take the Metro), but you might put those dollars toward buying an "official portrait" of your child or even your whole family in the Oval Office.

MEDIEVAL TIMES DINNER & TOURNAMENT

Young ladies and lords have a regal time at this replica of a castle from the Middle Ages cast in the most modern of settings—a shopping mall.

43

Dine on an authentic medieval four-course feast while valiant knights on horseback compete in games of skill and jousting during a live two-hour performance.

Like any gracious host and hostess, the king and princess greet each guest upon arrival. Everyone receives a crown in a color that determines which of six knights you'll cheer for and where you'll dine in the 1,020-seat arena organized by colors. If you child has a color preference, let the staff know.

Some children may actually follow the plot during the two-hour performance. The king seeks revenge for the prince's death, a princess looks for love, and a wizard named Cedric warns of betrayal. Horses dance to waltzlike music. But for most boys and girls, the storyline is secondary to the action.

KEEP IN MIND If your child is afraid of the dark, you might want to skip Medieval Times since a lot of the action takes place in semi-darkness. Take I–95 north to exit 43A (Route 100 East) to exit 10A, Arundel Mills Boulevard. From the Baltimore–Washington Parkway, proceed to Arundel Mills Boulevard. Medieval Times is in Arundel Mills Mall.

MAKE THE MOST OF YOUR TIME Medieval Times encourages guests to arrive one hour early. This gives you time to get crowned and browse in the gift shop (full of temptations like wooden swords, and costumes for squires and princesses). The Torture Chamber is small and definitely not for young children. But the $2 cover charge may be worth the price of admission for some preteens and teenagers who may be so grossed out by the replicas of these ancient devices that losing time on electronic toys or being grounded for a day would seem like a relatively mild punishment.

7000 Arundel Mills Circle,
Hanover, MD (Arundel Mills Mall)

888/935–6878;
www.medievaltimes.com

$54.95, $34.95 (12 and under), 3 and under sitting on laps free (taxes and gratuities not included)

W–Th 7, F 7:30, Sa 4 and 7, Su 5 (more shows may be available); gift shop open mall hrs

4 and up

Everyone is encouraged to root for their knights, and the crowd becomes boisterous as the battle begins. Knights on and off horses compete to become the champion. Although the swords aren't sharp, they create sparks when they clash, and the stunts are real. With swords, axes, spears, shields, and even hand-to-hand combat, knights duke it out with one another.

Notice the accuracy as the knights throw lances to one another while riding on the horses. They train by tossing water balloons back and forth! Maybe you'd be surprised to learn that some of the knights were recruited for their athleticism and didn't know how to ride horses. They start as squires and train for 8 to 12 months before becoming knighted by the king.

If you like this sight, you might also like riding horses at Rock Creek Park (#19), the only place to ride in the city.

EATS FOR KIDS Although this experience may seem royal, don't expect your kids to act too fine and fancy as they eat. They can't. Just as in the middle ages, they don't dine with silverware here either. All four courses are finger food, except for the soup, which you drink out of the bowl. Everyone is served the same fare regardless of age or preference. So if your kid wouldn't like the creamy tomato bisque, garlic bread, chicken, spare ribs, and herb-basted potato, you might want to factor in a trip to the Mall's food court. Also, the beverage choices are limited to soda, tea, and water.

MOUNT VERNON

How much does your child know about our first president? Chances are not as much as you did when you were a kid. The people at Mount Vernon want to change that. A visit to Mount Vernon offers much more than a chance to see George Washington's elegant and stately mansion. In 2006 the Ford Orientation Center and the Donald W. Reynolds Museum and Education Center opened, so visitors get to know the Washington who was not just a soldier, but an entrepreneur, a stepfather, and even a kid. After purchasing a ticket, start at the orientation center, which features Mount Vernon in Miniature. With a step up on the platform, even preschoolers can watch with everyone else as drawers open, windows open, and fireplaces glow in this exact replica of the mansion.

During the 30-minute tour of the mansion, interpreters tell about Washington's home and answer questions, and give you a sense of the country's first president. Be sure to tell your children to look up on the ceiling in the first room to find pictures of farm tools. Upstairs, the beds may look small, but that's an optical illusion resulting from their being high off

MAKE THE MOST OF YOUR TIME There's so much to do, see, and learn here. You could easily spend a day here and not get bored. Mount Vernon is the most popular historic home in the country. Tourists pull up by the busload in spring and summer. To avoid the crowds, you could arrive late in the afternoon, but remember that the grounds close at 5. No matter what time of year you visit Mount Vernon, pick up an Adventure Map.

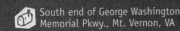 South end of George Washington
Memorial Pkwy., Mt. Vernon, VA

 $15 ages 12 and up,
$7 children 6–11

 Mar, Sept, and Oct, daily 9–5; Apr–Aug,
daily 8–5; Nov–Feb, daily 9–4

 703/780–2000;
www.mountvernon.org

 3 and up

the ground. The shortest mattress is 6'3", a tad longer than the general himself. Perhaps more interesting to kids than the house are a dozen meticulously restored outbuildings, including a major greenhouse, a kitchen, stables, and slave quarters.

The new Education Center is well worth the extra time. Sixteen galleries roughly follow a chronological view of Washington's life. Kids especially enjoy the animated cartoon of Washington's early life, Washington's false teeth, life-size images of Washington, and the movie in the "First in War Gallery," where the action on the screen is enhanced by falling snow, rumble seats, and fog.

For the child who must touch everything visit the Hands-on History room, where kids can play games and dress up.

If you like Mount Vernon, you may also like the Washington Monument (#6).

KEEP IN MIND The film "We Fight to be Free" in the Ford Orientation Center offers a wonderful overview of the estate and George Washington, but if your child is under 6 or afraid of loud noises, you won't want to stay past the first 15 minutes.

EATS FOR KIDS To protect Mount Vernon from damage and litter, food and beverages are not permitted on the grounds, but water fountains are near the mansion and all restrooms. Popcorn (that George Washington ate), pizza (which he didn't), and more are available in the **food court pavilion** with indoor and outdoor seating in the Reynolds building. For a taste of Colonial life, try Colonial Turkey Pye (made of turkey and mixed veggies topped with a homemade buttermilk biscuit) or peanut and chestnut soup at the **Mount Vernon Inn** (tel. 703/780–0011). The inn also offers modern meals, such as chicken fingers and hamburgers for kids.

MYSTICS BASKETBALL

4

Kids don't need a wizard's wand or sorcerer's stone to enjoy the magic of the Mystics, Washington's popular WNBA team. Adults don't need a wad of money either. At a fraction of what it costs to watch the Wizards (Washington's NBA team), you can catch a family-friendly Mystics game at the Verizon Center, the 20,000-seat arena at the crossroads of Metro's red, green, and yellow lines.

Women have come a long way since they first dribbled basketballs in 1892, a year after the game was invented and nearly three decades before they won the vote. People could have hardly imagined a women's professional basketball league back in the early 1890s, when women wore floor-length dresses, even on the court. They gained more freedom in 1896, when they began playing in bloomers, loose-fitting trousers gathered at the knee. Now, of course, they, like men, dress for comfort and ease of motion when they play, sweating through plenty of socks (around 960!) each season.

MAKE THE MOST OF YOUR TIME Gather a group of 20 or more and you not only qualify for discount tickets, you can have your group's message, such as "Happy Birthday" or "Congratulations," highlighted on the telescreen. You don't even need to plan far in advance. A day's notice (tel. 202/527–7518) is all you need!

EATS FOR KIDS Eat at the game or stroll under the gold-and-red arch to Chinatown. The noodle chef entertains folks as he stretches dough into strips of pasta from the front window of **Chinatown Express** (746 6th St. NW, tel. 202/638–0424). Order your noodles with beef, chicken, or seafood. Or slurp them in a soup. **Tony Cheng's** (619 H St. NW, tel. 202/371–8669) offers barbecue on the first floor and traditional fare upstairs.

 601 F St. NW. Metro:
Gallery Place/Chinatown

 202/527-7540, www.washingtonmystics.com;
Verizon Center, 202/661-5050, 877/DC HOOP,
www.verizoncenter.com

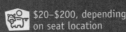 $20–$200, depending
on seat location

 Memorial Day–Labor Day,
many games weekends

 5 and up

During the game, a panda named Pax and 25 Mayhem dancers, ages 7–18, cheer on the players and spread high-fives through the crowd. (Just think: 600 kids try out for the Mayhem.) During the game, other kids give out bangers (long balloons that when clapped together create a thunderous sound) that add to the excitement.

Need another reason to see the Mystics? Tickets are easier to come by than for the Verizon Center's other teams, the Wizards and Capitals of the NHL.

If you like the Mystics, you might also like another testament to the power of women at the National Museum of Women in the Arts (#26).

KEEP IN MIND If you ever come for a Capitals game, you might want to visit the Hockey 101 booth, where team representatives answer your questions. For example, how many sticks do the players use? Some players may go through a couple per game, while others use one for a whole season. How do players sharpen their skates? They don't. The equipment manager sharpens them. If your kids are too young to ask questions, they might enjoy a hug from Slapshot, the Capitals' mascot. With a wingspan of 6 feet, this eagle can tickle your kids with his feathers.

NATIONAL AIR AND SPACE MUSEUM

40

There's a good reason why this place is the most popular museum in the world: Kids love it. The 22 galleries here tell the story of aviation and space from the earliest human attempts at flight. Suspended from the ceiling like plastic models in a child's room are dozens of aircraft, including the actual 1903 Wright Flyer that Orville Wright piloted over the sands of Kitty Hawk, Charles Lindbergh's *Spirit of St. Louis,* the X-1 rocket plane in which Chuck Yeager broke the sound barrier, and the X-15, the fastest aircraft ever built.

Kids like walking through the backup model of the *Skylab* orbital workshop to see how astronauts live (in quarters as cramped as a child's messy bedroom). At the How Things Fly gallery, children sit in a real Cessna 150 cockpit, "perform" experiments in midair, and see wind-tunnel demonstrations. An activity board at the gallery entrance lists times for family favorites such as paper airplane contests and demonstrations by museum "Explainers," high school and college students who encourage kids to participate. At the Explore the Universe exhibit, kids learn how past stargazers mapped the heavens with telescopes, cameras, and spectroscopes and what mysteries about our universe still remain.

MAKE THE MOST OF YOUR TIME You're one in a million—make that 6 to 9 million (depending on the year)—annual visitors, that is. The world's most popular museum is also thought to be Earth's most visited building. The museum is also huge (three blocks) and popular. To avoid crowds, go early on a weekday morning or plan your visit for fall or winter. The tickets to film and planetarium shows sell out quickly, so buy your tickets on arrival (or in advance through the Web site).

Independence Ave. and 6th St. SW.
Metro: L'Enfant Plaza

202/633-1000 or 202/633-5285, 202/633-1729
TTY; theater, planetarium 877/932-4634 or
202/633-4629; www.nasm.si.edu

Free

Daily 10–5:30

3 and up

Don't let long lines deter you from seeing a show in the five-story Lockheed Martin IMAX Theater. Films like *To Fly!* (a kid's favorite) make you feel you've left the ground. Strollers aren't allowed at the movies, but kids under 4 may find the noise and larger-than-life images frightening anyway.

For a look at the final frontier, check out the Albert Einstein Planetarium. *Infinity Express,* a 20-minute tour of the universe and Cosmic Collisions, a film about the dynamic evolution of the universe are shown throughout the day. *The Stars Tonight,* for stargazers 6 and up, discusses at 10:30 AM what you can expect to see in the current sky (Tuesday, Thursday, and Saturday). Before you leave, go to Milestones of Flight to touch the moon rock, one of only three on the planet you can feel.

If you like this sight, you may also like the Steven F. Udvar-Hazy Center (#39).

KEEP IN MIND Consider dressing your children in identical colors so that you can spot them easily. Also, review safety rules ahead of time, and point out what the security officers are wearing (white shirts, navy slacks, and hats) so your children know whom to turn to if they get lost.

EATS FOR KIDS Take your place in the **cafeteria** line for a bite of the most familiar restaurant food on earth—McDonald's—plus offerings from Boston Market and Donatos Pizza. Upstairs you can look out on the Mall and the National Museum of the American Indian. If you want a treat to take home, head to the tri-level gift shop, which sells such flight-related merchandise as freeze-dried astronaut food.

NATIONAL AIR AND SPACE
MUSEUM'S STEVEN F. UDVAR-HAZY CENTER

L ike its older but smaller sibling (the Air and Space Museum on the Mall, *see* #40), the Steven F. Udvar-Hazy Center tells the story of aviation and space exploration with displays of aircraft and spacecraft. But this museum isn't divided into galleries. Instead, aircraft are displayed in huge hangars on three levels under a ceiling that's 10 stories high.

This gargantuan Smithsonian facility displays hundreds of aircraft, spacecrafts, rockets, satellites, and experimental flying machines, including a Concorde, the Space Shuttle *Enterprise,* the fabled Lockheed SR-71 *Blackbird,* which in 1990 flew from Los Angeles to Washington, D.C., in slightly more than an hour, and the *Enola Gay,* which in 1944 dropped on Japan the first atomic devices to be used in war.

KEEP IN MIND Check out the Discovery Carts throughout the center. You might just get to try on replicas of $20,000 space gloves while younger children can play with astronaut dolls. You also might learn how astronauts take care of elimination issues. (Think diapers.)

When you enter the building, you'll be in the Boeing Aviation Hangar, with civil aviation to the left and military aviation to the right. Straight ahead you'll see the Space Shuttle *Enterprise.*

MAKE THE MOST OF YOUR TIME There's a $15 fee to park your car in the gigantic parking lot right in front of the museum. You really don't have any other parking options so be prepared to pay the fee. The only way around it is to visit after 4 when parking is free. Other expenses might include an IMAX movie, a trip on a flight simulator, and a souvenir from the gift shop.

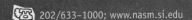

The museum's wide aisles and cement floors are ideal for strollers, and the planes are big enough that parents of toddlers don't have to hoist them up on their shoulders to see. (As a matter of fact, signs throughout the museum let you know that adults can't hold kids on their shoulders, for safety reasons.) Skywalks will take you nose-to-nose with the smaller aircraft suspended from the ceiling.

You can't miss the big stuff, but if you don't look carefully at the display cases, you might skip some unexpected treasures, such as space toys, memorabilia from the days of Lindbergh-mania, personal items the astronauts carried, and a space-traveling spider named Anita.

Before you leave, make sure you go to the Observation Tower. Here you can see planes taking off and landing at nearby Dulles International Airport and a panoramic view of Northern Virginia.

If you like this sight, you may also like the National Air and Space Museum (#40) and the College Park Aviation Museum (#60).

EATS FOR KIDS Like at a small airport, your choices are limited here. On-site, you can find a McDonald's and a McCafé. To take off for more options, go down Route 50 where you can find local chain restaurants such as **Anita's** (13921 Lee Jackson Hwy., tel. 703/378–1717), with mini-tacos for kids, and national chains, such as **Bob Evans** (14050 Thunderbolt Pl., tel. 703/834–0511), where spaghetti is popular at lunch. But if you leave the site you can't reenter without paying for parking again, so you may want to plan your visit so it doesn't conflict with lunch or snack time.

NATIONAL AQUARIUM

The basement of the Department of Commerce building is a strange address for a tourist attraction, but that's where you can find the nation's oldest public aquarium. Since the 1870s, it has housed interesting sea creatures, including a two-headed diamond terrapin in the 1940s, whose two heads would compete for the same morsel of food. Although you won't see any two-headed creatures or huge sharks that make a big splash, this museum's small size is a plus for parents of tots young enough to enjoy a pet goldfish.

Unlike more modern aquariums, this one is small enough that you can circle through it in about 20 minutes. Aisles are wide enough for double strollers, and the aquarium isn't generally crowded. Nevertheless, more than 250 species and 1,500 specimens of aquatic life, including American alligators, spiny lobsters, venomous lionfish, clownfish, flesh-chomping piranhas, and their seaworthy mates swim here. Animals live in traditional rectangular tanks.

MAKE THE MOST OF YOUR TIME If the National Aquarium whets your appetite for fish, visit Baltimore's glitzier **National Aquarium** (Pier 3, tel. 410/576–3800; www.aqua.org). An hour's drive from D.C. off-peak, it's Maryland's top tourist attraction. But be warned: It's more expensive and crowded than Washington's aquarium.

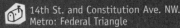

14th St. and Constitution Ave. NW.
Metro: Federal Triangle

$9 ages 11 and up,
$4 ages 3–10

Daily 9–5

202/482–2825;
www.nationalaquarium.com

1–7

The aquarium features habitats that represent the Office of National Marine Sanctuaries stretching from the Florida Keys to Fagatele Bay in American Samoa. Freshwater tanks focus on familiar friends such as turtles and newts, and a few unfamiliar fish, too. The boneytail chub, one of most rare fish in the Colorado River, is close to extinction because so many dams were built. This fish grows up to about two feet and may live more than 40 years.

Special events are held throughout the year. On Shark Day, you can watch a shark dissection. During Reptile Day, herpetologists (reptile experts) rave about these cold-blooded vertebrates. Did you know that American alligators have 80 cone-shaped teeth that they lose twice a year until they stop growing? They keep the tooth fairy—or shall we say tooth mermaid—busy!

If you like this sight, you may also like the National Zoo (#24).

KEEP IN MIND
At the cash register where you pay for your visit, they sell Adventure Pack bags with minislides of some of the creatures. Before you consider plunking down two bucks, you might want to check out the spacious gift shop where you can purchase necklaces with shark's teeth, T-shirts, stuffed seahorses, and more.

EATS FOR KIDS Sharks are fed at 2 on Monday, Wednesday, and Saturday. Piranhas are fed at 2 on Tuesday, Thursday, and Sunday. Alligators are fed at 2 on Friday. People can catch a bite to eat at any time at food courts in the lower level of the **Ronald Reagan Building** (1300 Pennsylvania Ave. NW, tel. 202/312–1300). On a pleasant day, consider walking over to the top level of the **Shops** (see the White House #2).

37

W here does your family keep its most precious papers? Our nation's most important documents are housed at the National Archives.

Here you can find the Declaration of Independence, the Constitution, and the Bill of Rights. If you think about it, it's rather extraordinary that our country puts these priceless papers on display to throngs of visitors who peer through protective glass for a glimpse of history. The glass is equipped with filters and filled with argon gas (it's colorless, odorless, and tasteless) to protect these irreplaceable documents from light and air, which fade and deteriorate ink and paper.

One of the most frequent questions kids ask about the National Archives concerns the 2004 award-winning movie *National Treasure,* starring Nicholas Cage. The film wasn't filmed inside the building but there are some shots of the outside of the building. In the movie, Cage's character steals the Declaration of Independence and finds a map on the backside. There isn't a map on the Declaration, but there is writing. It reads, ORIGINAL DECLARATION OF

EATS FOR KIDS If your child is hungry for more than knowledge, the **Charters Café** sells hot and cold sandwiches, snacks, and fresh fruit. Its walls are lined with vintage agricultural posters from the archive's collection that encourage healthful eating.

MAKE THE MOST OF YOUR TIME Unless you're visiting on a blustery day in February, be prepared to wait in line for at least 30 minutes. Start your visit while waiting in line. Call 202/357–6829 to hear an audio introduction to the Charters of Freedom and get the code to discounts at the Archives Gift Shop. While waiting outside, ask your child to count the columns (there are 72). While you're waiting to see the big three documents (the Declaration, the Constitution, and the Bill of Rights), ask your child to find three famous founders in the paintings—Thomas Jefferson, Benjamin Franklin, and George Washington. For clear copies of the documents, visit the gift shop.

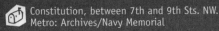 Constitution, between 7th and 9th Sts. NW.
Metro: Archives/Navy Memorial

 202/357-5000, www.archives.gov; Reservations
recommended in the spring and summer at
www.recreation.gov or 877/444-6777

 Free

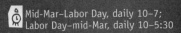 Mid-Mar–Labor Day, daily 10–7;
Labor Day–mid-Mar, daily 10–5:30

 7 and up

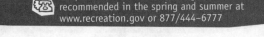

INDEPENDENCE, DATED 4TH JULY 1776, and it appears upside down on the bottom of the document. Although you can't see the flipside of the Declaration, other objects in the archive's vast collection that may interest kids include immigration records, treaties, and recordings of Teddy Roosevelt's voice. You can even make your own Great Seal, guess the use of a patent, and create your own documentary film.

Budding architects might notice a similarity between this building and the west wing of the National Gallery of Art (*see* #34), the Thomas Jefferson Memorial (*see* #13), and the DAR Constitution Hall (*see* #58). John Russell Pope designed them all in a neoclassical-revival style.

If you like this sight, you might also like seeing the signatures of the signers of the Declaration carved into a stone wall at Constitution Gardens, near the Vietnam Veterans Memorial.

KEEP IN MIND The Declaration wasn't always stored and displayed safely behind glass at the National Archives for millions of people to view. It has had many homes, including government offices, the interiors of safes, and other public displays. Wagons, ships, a Pullman sleeper, and an armored vehicle have transported this priceless document.

NATIONAL BUILDING MUSEUM

The Big Bad Wolf won't blow this house down! More than 15 million bricks make up this building, designed by Civil War veteran Montgomery Meigs and constructed from 1882 to 1887. The inside of the building will awe budding builders and architects. The Great Hall, site of many inaugural balls, is 15 stories tall and is as long as a football field. Eight 75-foot Corinthian columns are among the world's largest. Although they look like marble, each is made of 70,000 bricks, covered with plaster and marbleized.

For kids who have transitioned from tearing down towers of blocks to building their own, the Building Zone is a safe place for both. Designed for kids ages 2 to 6, the Zone has a dress-up section with hard hats, tool belts, and goggles for kids who want to look like Bob the Builder. On weekends, your children (and you) can learn how bridges work and how buildings, for the most part, manage to stay in one piece.

MAKE THE MOST OF YOUR TIME
Borrow a tool kit for $5 at the information desk. "Patterns: Here, There, and Everywhere" for kids 3 to 7 has stamps and rubbings and games for learning about brick patterns, "Eye Spy: What Can you Find With Your Little Eye?" for kids 7 to 10 includes jigsaw puzzles and create your own postcards, and "Constructor Detector" for kids 8 to 11 includes a scavenger hunt and supplies to create a pattern that you can take home as a souvenir.

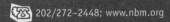

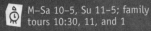

In the Washington: Symbol and City exhibit, children can handle plastic models of the Capitol, White House, Washington Monument, and Lincoln Memorial. Special exhibits change as often as five times per year, but all focus on the people, processes, or materials that create buildings and other "places." Recent exhibits have explored the art of Lego building, parking garages, and elevators, escalators, and moving sidewalks.

Every day the museum has other drop-in activities, most of which are free. And with the free Treasure Hunt (kids 6 and up) and Adventures in Architecture (for preteens) booklets from the Information Desk, you and your kids can explore some of the nooks and crannies of this cool building.

If you like this sight, you may also like Washington National Cathedral (#5), the sixth largest cathedral in the world, which took less than a century to build.

EATS FOR KIDS
When appetites build, visit **FireHook Bakery** (tel. 202/628–0906) in the museum for handcrafted and prepackaged sandwiches, salads, and desserts. Eat in or take your lunch to go and sit at the benches across the street at the National Law Enforcement Officers Memorial, a tribute to officers killed in the line of duty.

KEEP IN MIND Extensive school programs (also available to other groups, like scout troops) complement curricula in social studies, science, art, math, and history. Under the guidance of the museum's educators, students may plan an imaginary town, build model bridges, or assemble an 8' x 11' house from the ground up with foundations, wall frames, and trusses. Most programs cost a dollar or two for each student. For information, call the museum's education department. Check out the museum store, known as one of the best museum shops in D.C., for take-home building supplies.

NATIONAL CAPITAL TROLLEY MUSEUM

What small child doesn't love trains? And what small child who loves trains doesn't love trolleys? You can test this hypothesis at this combination trolley trip and museum. The 20-minute voyage covers 1¾ mi of track through a wooded area. Often, passengers see deer, fox, rabbits, and groundhogs, but kids are usually content just watching the trolley itself.

Also called streetcars, trolleys were first used in Washington, D.C., during the Lincoln administration to accommodate the influx of people during the Civil War. Early streetcars were drawn by horses, but these were replaced by cable cars and ultimately by electric cars, which skimmed quickly and smoothly along the tracks. The last Washington trolleys ran during the Kennedy administration. In fact, you might be riding in one of these last cars or in a car from another country. The museum's collection comprises 12 cars, which are all brought out on the third Sunday in April for the Cavalcade of Cars and the third Sunday in October for the Fall Open House. Both events also feature other attractions,

MAKE THE MOST OF YOUR TIME Your trolley ticket makes a good souvenir. Each conductor uses a hole punch with a different shape—perhaps a star or zigzag. When the trolleys were in use, the holes helped identify conductors in case a passenger complained.

EATS FOR KIDS Food and drink aren't allowed in the museum or on the cars. Families can be choosy at the Layhill Shopping Center (Layhill and Bel Pre Rds.), where they'll find Italian fare and video games at **Sole d' Italia**, run by the same family since 1974 (tel. 301/598–6660), Chinese food at **Lee's Kitchen** (tel. 301/598–4810), a **McDonald's**, and a **Subway**.

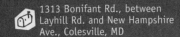 1313 Bonifant Rd., between Layhill Rd. and New Hampshire Ave., Colesville, MD

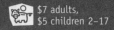 $7 adults, $5 children 2–17

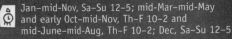 Jan–mid-Nov, Sa–Su 12–5; mid-Mar–mid-May and early Oct–mid-Nov, Th–F 10–2 and mid-June–mid-Aug, Th–F 10–2; Dec, Sa–Su 12–5

 301/384–6088; www.dctrolley.org

 2–7 and all train lovers

such as a barbershop quartet. During December's Holly Trolleyfest, Santa greets children during the ride.

Also take time to enjoy this small museum, which reopened in a new building in 2010. With a boost, even the smallest child can crank a handle to send a model trolley whizzing around in a case depicting Connecticut Avenue in the early 1930s. Older kids and parents can learn the parts of a trolley and the history of D.C. trolleys through interactive computers.

Trolley memorabilia, *Thomas the Tank Engine* books, and other train-related merchandise are available in the shop. A free "Little Folks Guide to the Trolley Museum" handout and the trolley tickets themselves make nice mementos that can be used to play trolley at home.

If your family likes this museum, you might also like the College Park Aviation Museum (#60), a site devoted to air transportation.

KEEP IN MIND The biggest trolley trick for parents of toddlers is keeping them safely seated during the short ride. Luckily, the trolley makes one stop en route, when kids can get up and walk around. This is also when enthusiastic volunteers give brief trolley talks and answer questions. Often some of the passengers will remember riding the trolley when they were kids.

NATIONAL GALLERY OF ART
AND SCULPTURE GARDEN

Some kids think it looks like a bird, others a plane, but most agree it's super. Looming as large as a small aircraft, a mobile by Alexander Calder soars overhead in the East Building atrium here. It's just one of the works that fascinates kids at this art museum, one of the world's most visited. The gallery comprises two very different buildings and a sculpture garden. The airy and spacious East Building's modern art—by Picasso, Matisse, Miró, and others—appeals to children, as does the exterior of the I. M. Pei–designed trapezoidal structure. In fact, since its 1978 opening, the bladelike southwest corner has been darkened and polished smooth by thousands of hands irresistibly drawn to touch it.

In the neoclassical West Building, more than 100 galleries contain 13th- to 19th-century works. Though art lovers easily spend all day here, most little children last about an hour. (Strollers are available at both buildings' entrances.) Students of architecture may notice that the building's dome shape resembles the Jefferson Memorial. Both buildings were designed by John Russell Pope and opened in the early 1940s.

MAKE THE MOST OF YOUR TIME Free weekend Family Work-
shops (registration required; call up to three weeks in advance) include tours and activities.
If you'd rather go it alone, start in the Information Room in the West Building to preview
works by computer. Or you may rent the Adventures in Art family audio tour, which explores
Dutch and Flemish paintings ($3 per tour, $2 for extra headphones, ages 7–12).

4th St. and Constitution Ave. NW, East Building;
6th and Constitution, NW, West Building.
Metro: Judiciary Square, Archives, Smithsonian

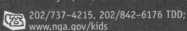 202/737–4215, 202/842–6176 TDD;
www.nga.gov/kids

 Free

 M–Sa 10–5, Su 11–6

 4 and up

Even the littlest tots enjoy the sculpture garden. The massive *Spider* by Louise Bourgeois is large enough to frighten even the bravest Miss Muffet. The rabbit *Thinker on a Rock* by Barry Flanagan can promote a discussion about other famous rabbits. Ask your child, "What do you suppose it's thinking about?" The only sculpture kids (or adults) can touch is Scott Burton's *Six-Part Seating,* with its polished granite chairs. Still, the meandering paths reveal unexpected treasures, such as Roy Lichtenstein's *House I.* Claes Oldenburg and Coosje van Bruggen's mammoth *Typewriter Eraser, Scale X* looks foreign to kids. Ask your kids to guess what it is.

If your family likes this sight, they may also like the Phillips Collection (#20).

KEEP IN MIND

When it's too cold to enjoy the sculpture garden, toddlers might enjoy the moving walkway in the underground tunnel connecting the East and West buildings. But for older kids in the winter, there's more to do here than see artwork. Ice-skating is offered mid-March through mid-November, weather permitting.

EATS FOR KIDS Some people skip the art and go straight for the gelato (19 flavors in all) at the **Espresso Bar**. In the West Building, the **Garden Café** (tel. 202/712–7460; reservations recommended for groups of more than eight) features American fare. Or why not pick up a pizza or a sandwich outside at the sculpture garden's **Pavilion Café** and sit on one of the camel-back sofas?

NATIONAL GEOGRAPHIC MUSEUM

The National Geographic Society's famous yellow-bordered magazine—found in doctors' offices, family rooms, and attics nationwide—is not exactly for kids. Yet the Society's museum brings the planet's wonders closer and shows kids that it is indeed a small world after all.

Exhibits rotate here just as the moon and Earth do. Displays vary, just like the magazine's features. Dinosaurs, glowing worms and mutant fireflies, modern mapping with a 10-foot globe, the *March of the Penguins* movie with a live appearance from these live flightless birds, and King Tut's mummified remains have all been studied in depth here. One exhibit about what scientists have learned from "Crittercams" (data collecting devices worn by the animals) had kids crawling through a tunnel and pop up in a bubble to come face-to-face with a penguin wearing a working Crittercam.

KEEP IN MIND Through magazines, TV, radio, maps, books, CD-ROMs, and the Internet, the National Geographic Society brings the world to more than 300 million people worldwide. You can find many of the Society's publications in the gift shop, including National Geographic Kids, the magazine for 6- to 14-year-olds.

MAKE THE MOST OF YOUR TIME The good news is that the exhibits here are well-researched, very visual, modern, and when they're for families, very fun. The bad news is that there's a chance that the current exhibits might not be appropriate for all ages. Exhibits change about every three to six months, so check the Web site or call before you visit.

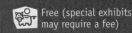
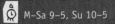
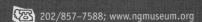

Kids can ham it up and see their faces on the cover of *National Geographic*. Postcard-size pictures ($5) can be made at In the Picture, where they can choose their own backgrounds—among 12 scenes such as tulips outside the White House, the Great Wall of China, Mount Everest, or even the moon. Other props include furry creatures like panda bears, tigers, or gorillas.

You can walk outside the museum's portico and peer through the glass 365 days of the year, 24 hours a day, to see relief maps created with satellite imagery and artifacts from past expeditions. You can watch and listen to the National Geographic channel or check out the electronic ticker tape, which, not unexpectedly, tells about the latest expeditions, adventures, and discoveries in science and geography.

If you like this sight, you may also like the Newseum (#23).

EATS FOR KIDS In a neighborhood catering to businesspeople, you won't find high chairs, but you will find reasonable prices. In addition to a Quiznos, Potbelly, and Subway nearby, the self-service **California Grill** (1720 M St. NW, tel. 202/463–4200) specializes in Mexican and American cuisine and the **Mudd House** (1724 M St. NW, tel. 202/822–8455) offers a place for parents to sip specialty coffees while kids warm up with hot chocolate.

NATIONAL HARBOR

When the **National Children's Museum** opens in 2013, this waterfront destination of hotels, restaurants, and shops should be just as popular for kids as it is for convention attendees. Designated by Congress, the 150,000-square-foot museum will focus on six topics: the environment, civic engagement, the arts, health, world cultures, and play. But until construction is complete, there's an assortment of the other amusements in the harbor to amuse kids. For a free mini-preview of the new museum in a small space, check out the **Launch Zone** (112 Water St., tel. 301/686–0225; www.ncm.museum).

Take a picture (everyone else does) of your children giving high-fives to a hand more than 100 times larger than their own, sliding down a huge leg, or sitting in a monstrous mouth and living to tell about it. Or better yet, join in and climb all over *The Awakening*, the immense statue of a man who is half-buried in the ground. Transplanted from D.C.'s East Potomac Park, J. Seward Johnson's *The Awakening* reminds some kids of dad when he's waking up. Others think he looks like a monster. Directly in front of *The Awakening*,

MAKE THE MOST OF YOUR TIME National Harbor isn't near D.C. attractions or a Metro rail station, and parking can be just as expensive here as it is downtown.

EATS FOR KIDS Chicken tenders are easy to find as almost all of the two dozen restaurants in the Harbor have kids' menus. **McLoone's Pier House** (141 National Harbor, tel. 732/212–9910) and **McCormick & Schmick's** (145 National Plaza, tel. 301/567–6224) are both part of national chains that are typical here.

 National Harbor, MD 20745

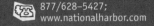 877/628-5427;
www.nationalharbor.com

 Varies

 Every day

 3 and up

the first (and so far only) **Peeps & Company** (150 National Dr., tel. 301/749-5791; www.justborn. com) sells their signature mushy marshmallow Easter treats and other candies.

Fireworks, free movies, and water taxis to D.C. and Mount Vernon (*see* #42) add to National Harbor's appeal in the summer, but winter might be the best time to visit. From mid-November through the first week in January, the **Gaylord Hotel** (201 Waterfront St., tel. 301/965-2000; www.gaylordhotels.com) hosts a winter wonderland called ICE! Sculptors hand-carve winter scenes of Washington, the North Pole, a toyland, and more. Despite the nine-degree temperature inside (parkas given out at the door help ease the chill), many kids think it's quite nice or, shall we say, quite ice!

If you like this sight, you may also like Six Flags America (#16).

KEEP IN MIND In 2009 Walt Disney bought a 15-acre site at National Harbor to build a hotel in the Harbor. It will join Aloft, Gaylord National Resort, Hampton Inn & Suites, Residence Inn by Marriott, Westin, and Wyndham.

NATIONAL MUSEUM OF AFRICAN ART

Kids can really relate to the art at this museum. Perhaps it's because every child has turned a paper plate into a mask or strung beads together to make a necklace. Perhaps it's because so many of the works incorporate animals. Wander through this Smithsonian museum with your child, and you can see all sorts of African artworks: musical instruments, pottery, beaded works, sculptures, carvings, and masks and headdresses made to entertain or personify characters or animals. Jewelry on display is made of such materials as beads, woods, fiber, bronze, ivory, and fired clay.

One of the best ways to learn about the arts and cultures of Africa is through the AfriKid Art programs, aimed at kids 4 and up. At drop-in workshops (most of which are free), children are taught about the materials, colors, animals, and countries of origin of items in the permanent collection, such as a colorful beaded crown or a life-size figure of a man. They may also be asked to answer questions like, "How would you describe the object to someone who couldn't see it?" or "How do you think it would feel to wear this hat?" After

MAKE THE MOST OF YOUR TIME To expand your children's global view even further, walk about 100 paces west through the Enid A. Haupt Garden or just open the door at the end of the Art of the Personal Object gallery, and you'll be in the Sackler Gallery (*see #17*), which is connected to the Freer Gallery of Art. The emphasis at these nearby museums is on another continent altogether: Asia.

950 Independence Ave. SW.
Metro: Smithsonian

202/633-1000, 202/357-1729 TTY;
www.nmafa.si.edu

Free

Daily 10–5:30

4 and up

touring the gallery, kids pursue an activity, such as beading, weaving, or hat making, and can take their masterpiece home as a souvenir.

To help in your exploration, consider counting the number of masks or musical instruments in the gallery.

The museum also has storytelling sessions, during which folktales are often combined with music and dance to bring legends from the African continent to life. And in the true tradition of African storytelling, the audience frequently chimes in.

If you like this sight, you may also like the National Museum of Women in Arts (#26).

KEEP IN MIND The gift shop, like all Smithsonian stores, doesn't charge any sales tax. Chances are you'll see some cool items here, including animals made from beads, wood, and even old soda cans. You might even find chocolate bars from Ghana.

EATS FOR KIDS Pick up fresh fruit, bread, and more on Friday from June through September at the Farmers Market in the parking lot outside the Department of Agriculture (12th St. and Independence Ave.). Check out the food at the National Air and Space Museum, the National Museum of Natural History, the National Museum of the American Indian, and the National Museum of American History have on-site restaurants.

NATIONAL MUSEUM OF AMERICAN HISTORY

Oh say, can you see the flag that inspired "The Star-Spangled Banner," Kermit the Frog, an original teddy bear from 1903, first ladies' inaugural gowns, and a five-story dollhouse? You can, and you can see lots more American memorabilia on three floors of exhibitions, whose incredible diversity of artifacts gave it the nickname "the nation's attic," but this phrase no longer fits. After an $85 million renovation, this museum is as well organized as if it were new.

If you're with train-loving tots, head to the first floor to see the big rigs. Exhibits on the first floor emphasize the history of science and technology and include farm machines, antique automobiles, and a 260-ton steam locomotive. "America on the Move" starts in 1856 as the railroad comes to a California town and ends in 1999 in Los Angeles, the "Ellis Island of the end of the 20th century" as pilgrims arrive from other countries daily. Maybe your children will follow the 14 historical settings in chronological order, but chances are they'll zip through pointing out the 1939 Dodge school bus painted "double deep"

KEEP IN MIND This museum brings American history to life for kids of all ages. In "The American Presidency: A Glorious Burden," you can see the wooden lap desk that Thomas Jefferson designed and used to draft the Declaration of Independence. Also check out George Washington's sword and Abraham Lincoln's top hat.

MAKE THE MOST OF YOUR TIME If you bring a purse or other bag with you, allow a little extra time for security. SparkLab! is divided into sections. Blocks and toys may keep toddlers busy while their older siblings participate in science experiments with Smithsonian staff and volunteers. But whether children are 2 or 10, they need to be with an adult in Spark!Lab.

 14th St. and Constitution Ave. NW.
Metro: Smithsonian, Federal Triangle

 Free

 Daily 10–5:30; Hands-On Science
T–F 12:30–5, Sa–Su 10–5.

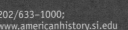 202/633–1000;
www.americanhistory.si.edu

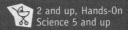 2 and up, Hands-On
Science 5 and up

orange; the toy ride-in car; and the 1955 station wagon with wood paneling. Look for "Bud," the official mascot of the exhibit, and his signs designed to stimulate family discussion about the exhibit. Two *Jurassic Park* eggs and an orange-masked Teenage Mutant Ninja Turtle are in the Science in American Life exhibit on the first floor.

The second floor, devoted to U.S. social and political history, even contains a house. Within These Walls follows the lives of families who lived at 16 Elm Street in Ipswich, Massachusetts, from the mid-1760s through 1945. The third floor's National Treasures of Popular Culture rotates displays familiar items, like Dorothy's ruby slippers in the *Wizard of Oz*. For a more interactive visit, children and adults should stop at the Spark!Lab. Kids unravel the mysteries of DNA, conduct tests for water pollutants as scientists did in the 1880s, and become "Star-Spangled Banner" conservators.

If you like this sight, you may also like the National Museum of Natural History (#27), next door.

EATS FOR KIDS If your kids scream for ice cream, visit the museum's Constitution Café and gelato bar (first floor, Constitution Avenue entrance) for an Italian treat. For more options, the Stars and Stripes Café on the lower level serves all-American barbeque, pizza, sandwiches, burgers, salads and dessert. When the weather is good, grab a hot dog from the food carts and picnic outside.

NATIONAL MUSEUM OF
THE AMERICAN INDIAN

Your introduction to American Indian life and indeed U.S. history begins before you enter this Smithsonian museum that opened in 2004. Plants that were native to the area before European settlers arrived grow in an upland hardwood forest, lowland freshwater wetlands, and a meadow. Crops known as the "three sisters"—corn, beans, and squash—will also grow. Cascading water represents purification and a nurturing spirit. Even the building's stone-clad forms reflect the wearing by wind and water over time.

Above the information desk, look and listen as the words and sounds at the Welcome Wall come from languages of Native people from the northern tip of the Arctic to the southern tip of South America. Then feel the cool copper bands woven into the wall representing traditions of textiles and basketry. Many weekends, American Indians demonstrate weaving, boat building, dancing, and drumming in the spacious Potomac Atrium. No matter what day you visit, look at the "light show" reflected from the prism window. When the sun is at its peak, from 11 AM to 2 PM, the sun's beams dance across the floors and walls.

KEEP IN MIND The two museum stores carry an impressive collection of books for children about Native American life, from the lovely legends of yesteryear to life today to folklore fantasies. In *Coyote in Love with a Star*, the famous trickster takes a job as a rodent control officer at the former World Trade Center in New York City. Through the "My World" book series, kids meet real Native American children. You can also pick up some authentic Native crafts here at reasonable prices. But a better reminder of your visit is free. Send a souvenir e-mail postcard home by visiting the resource center on the third floor.

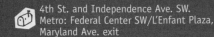
4th St. and Independence Ave. SW.
Metro: Federal Center SW/L'Enfant Plaza,
Maryland Ave. exit

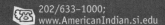
202/633-1000;
www.AmericanIndian.si.edu

Free

Daily 10-5:30

2 and up

Check out the floor-to-ceiling cases along the walls of the Window on Collections exhibits. Challenge your child to find the Inupiat school of fish carved from ivory, and the toy dolls in full regalia that are made from the hide of these massive beasts that can weigh more than 2,000 pounds.

The museum also helps explore old cultural myths. You've heard of cowboys and Indians. Well, some Native Americans were and are cowboys and cowgirls, too. They still ranch and entertain folks with their rodeo skills. Even children who have studied American Indians may be surprised to learn that more died from diseases brought from European settlers than from wars.

If like this sight, you may also like the planetarium shows at Rock Creek Park (#19) that include Native American legends about the stars.

MAKE THE MOST OF YOUR TIME

"Who We Are," a 3-minute presentation on the fourth floor, is a great introduction to contemporary Native life, but if your child covers her ears during thunderstorms, it might be wise to skip it.

EATS FOR KIDS Watch salmon being cooked over a fire pit built into the floor of the museum's **Mitsitam Native Foods Cafe.** Mitsitam means "Let's Eat" in the language of the Delaware and Piscataway. If your kids do not care for salmon, they probably like turkey. Choose from food native to five geographic regions: Northern Woodlands, South America, Northwest Coast, Meso-American, and the Great Plains. Whatever region's cuisine you select, try to get a seat at the window where it looks as if the water outside disappears under your feet.

Boys and girls who want real goose bumps or who have an interest in a medical career can find lots of really cool stuff at this medical museum that depicts the fight against injury and disease. Because some of the exhibits are fairly graphic, the museum will be perfect for those fond of the word "gross" but it may be unsuitable for the squeamish.

At the exhibit called *Visibly Human: Health and Disease,* kids explore how the body works, in sickness and in health. Compare a smoker's lung to a coal miner's lung, view a brain still attached to a spinal cord, and see the mega-colon. Some organs are "plastinated"—preserved in plastic so they can be touched—and injected with blue and red dyes so arteries can be distinguished from veins. All are real.

This place is full of bizarre stuff and stories. During the Battle of Gettysburg, a 12-pound cannonball splintered the right leg of Civil War General Daniel E. Sickles. After it was amputated, he sent the leg to this museum, then known as the Army Medical Museum,

KEEP IN MIND
Adults need to show a photo ID to gain entry to Walter Reed. Free parking is available in the driveway in front of the museum. On weekends, there are more open spaces near the museum.

MAKE THE MOST OF YOUR TIME
Docents lead tours of the museum on the second and fourth Saturday of every month at 1. Tours last 1–1½ hours and are recommended for ages 11 and up. Most docents focus on Civil War medicine. If you call ahead, the docents will bring out plastinated organs for you to feel. To keep *your* organs healthy, many docents share a tip unknown to Civil War physicians, who spread a lot of germs: wash your hands.

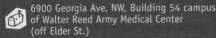
6900 Georgia Ave. NW, Building 54 campus
of Walter Reed Army Medical Center
(off Elder St.)

202/782-2200;
www.nmhm.washingtondc.museum

Free

Daily 10-5:30

9 and up

where it's still on display, along with a picture of the general as an amputee. Incidentally, the eccentric General Sickles used to visit his leg here and would sometimes bring friends to see it.

At other exhibits, your children can learn about the evolution of the microscope, discover the development of the human embryo, view the human body from a 3-D perspective, look at early medical instruments used in skull surgery, see Revolutionary War hero Paul Revere's dental tools (yes, he was famous for more than his midnight ride!), and discover why disease killed more soldiers than bullets during the Civil War. The most famous object on display is the bullet that killed President Lincoln (*see* Ford's Theatre #55). There's much here to make everyone grateful for modern medicine.

If you like this sight, you may also like the United States Botanic Garden (#12), with its medicinal plants.

EATS FOR KIDS For great selection and low prices, walk to the **Walter Reed Hospital Cafeteria** (Bldg. 2, tel. 202/782-2027). Or select a sandwich from **Subway** (also in Bldg. 2). **Burger King** is in building 1. Or drive a mile and a half for seafood at **Crisfield** (8012 Georgia Ave., Silver Spring, tel. 301/589-1306) served in a casual atmosphere with swivel chairs for teens and booster seats for little ones.

NATIONAL MUSEUM OF NATURAL HISTORY

Say hello to Henry. One of the largest elephants ever found in the world, this beast has greeted generations of kids in the rotunda of this huge Smithsonian museum, which is dedicated to natural wonders of the world, both big and small.

In the popular Dinosaur Hall, fossilized skeletons range from a 90-foot-long diplodocus to a tiny *Thesalorsaurus neglectus* (so named because its bones sat for years in a museum drawer before being reassembled). Cross the Rotunda (from the Dinosaur Hall) to the Hall of Mammals that features 274 creatures, including lions and tigers and bears, plus more exotic animals from the Australian tree kangaroos to a South American fairy armadillo. The star of the exhibit is a tiny, shrewlike creature, nicknamed "Morgie" for *Morganucodon oehleri*, one of the Earth's first mammals. Four-inch long Morgie foraged for food with dinosaurs 210 million years ago. A bronze sculpture depicts a slightly enlarged Morgie that is developing a shiny coat as kids pet their ancient ancestor.

MAKE THE MOST OF YOUR TIME Children explore with their hands in the Discovery Room. In the Discovery Center, you'll find the 487-seat Samuel C. Johnson Theater and its IMAX films. For 3-D flicks, you get to don oversize glasses. You won't need glasses to see the Dinosaur Hall's triceratops, on the first floor. Scientists studied this massive herbivore (plant eater) by scanning bones and using computers to make a life-like cast and video. Kids can compare it to what scientists in 1905 thought the triceratops looked like.

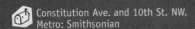 Constitution Ave. and 10th St. NW.
Metro: Smithsonian

 Free

 Daily 10–5:30; Discovery Room T–F 12–2:30, Sa–Su
10:30–3:30; Memorial Day–Labor Day, T–Su 10:30–30
(free passes may be required on busy days)

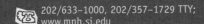 202/633–1000, 202/357–1729 TTY;
www.mnh.si.edu

2 and up, Discovery Room

Older children may enjoy the Janet Annenberg Hooker Hall of Geology, Gems & Minerals, which takes rock collecting to new heights and includes a neat exhibit on volcanoes and earthquakes. The Hope Diamond is also here; the most-visited museum object in the world, it's even more popular than the *Mona Lisa*. For a (literal) look at themselves, kids can merge pictures of themselves with images of our ancestors in the Hall of Human Origins, which opened in 2010. This 15,000-square-foot exhibit explores how humans evolved over 6 million years.

Not everything in the museum is dead or inanimate, though. For some action, take your kids to the second floor's O. Orkin Insect Zoo, home to live ants, bees, centipedes, tarantulas, roaches, and other critters you wouldn't want in your house. After viewing these creepy creatures, young bug fanciers can act the part by crawling through a model of an African termite mound.

If you like this sight, you may also like the National Zoo (#24).

KEEP IN MIND
In the Insect Zoo, roaches that freak out people are behind glass, but in the Butterfly Pavillion, winged insects freely fly overhead.

EATS FOR KIDS Tarantula feedings usually take place in the Insect Zoo at 10:30, 11:30, and 1:30 Tuesday through Friday and 11:30, 12:30, and 1:30 on weekends. Whereas the tarantulas' meal plan consists of the same old thing every day (crickets), you have lots of choices in the museum's 600-seat **Atrium Café** and the **Fossil Café**, where you eat at tables with little fossilized artifacts and illustrations under glass.

NATIONAL MUSEUM OF
WOMEN IN THE ARTS

Every day is International Women's Day at this beautifully restored 1908 Renaissance Revival building, showcasing works by prominent female artists from the Renaissance to the present. Ironically, it was once a men-only Masonic temple. Today, in addition to traveling shows, the museum houses a permanent collection, including paintings, drawings, sculpture, prints, and photographs by such artists as Mary Cassatt, Frida Kahlo, Gabriele Münter, and Helen Frankenthaler.

As at many art museums, it's not easy to know what children will like to see. Here there's actually a sculpture you can smell before you see it. Chakaia Booker's *Acid Rain* is made up of tons of tires. Nineteenth-century French artist Rosa Bonheur worked in a more traditional medium—paint—but her imaginative animal paintings, filled with rich and realistic textures, may also get kids talking. Teens may enjoy contrasting their practical clothes (some more practical than others) with the ornate Renaissance-era clothing of the young woman in Lavinia Fontana's *Portrait of a Noblewoman* (1580).

EATS FOR KIDS If your child will sit still for a fancy meal, stay in the museum for a bite to eat in the café. For more humble fare, the **Capitol City Brewing Company** (1100 New York Ave. NW, tel. 202/628–2222) serves mac 'n' cheese, crispy chicken, and meatloaf. **Haad Thai** (1100 New York Ave. NW, tel. 202/682–1111) offers kids crispy rolls and chicken on a skewer.

MAKE THE MOST OF YOUR TIME Once a year, the museum is transformed from formal to fun as women and men, girls and boys gather here for music, dancing, hands-on crafts, storytelling, and more at the museum's annual Family Festival. Usually celebrating another culture, the event is generally held in early spring, but the date varies because the festival is tied in with special exhibits. By October, the museum staff should be able to tell you when the next Family Festival will be held.

 1250 New York Ave. NW.
Metro: Metro Center

 202/783-5000;
www.nmwa.org

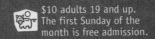 $10 adults 19 and up.
The first Sunday of the
month is free admission.

 M–Sa 10–5, Su 12–5

 6 and up

Free family programs for children and role-model workshops for teens are held about once a month. Reservations are required for most programs. The first Saturday of the month there's usually a program just for teens ages 13 and up. Woman artists teach techniques to groups of about 15 to 20 teens. Family programs, usually held on the first Sunday of the month, can usually accommodate groups of 40 kids.

At the information desk, pick up a brochure for kids (ages 6–10), which suggests ways to look at art through the elements of line, shape, color, and texture. Even though the artists covered at the museum are limited to women, the approach to art and the appeal to visitors are universal.

If you like this sight, you may also like the Corcoran Gallery of Art (#59), the city's oldest art museum.

KEEP IN MIND It's hard for many kids to understand why it's significant to have a museum that only displays art by women. To help kids understand, the staff may ask, "How many female artists can you name?" Here's one idea to get your child interested in the art here: Ask about bugs. When Maria Sibylla Merian (born 1647) was about 14 years old, she started collecting, studying, and drawing insects. You can see Maria Merian's highly descriptive etchings and watercolors at the museum.

NATIONAL POSTAL MUSEUM

This museum gets a stamp of approval!

Look up and see one of the first airmail planes. Then look around and you can see first-class opportunities for children at this Smithsonian-operated museum dedicated to the history of our mail service and stamps.

This Smithsonian museum is much smaller than its cousins on the National Mall. You can wander through in less than an hour.

Transportation-loving tots can pretend to move a lot of mail here. They can steer and push dozens of buttons on a full-size, big-rig truck cab right in the corner of the main exhibit area. Then they can experience what it was like to walk through the woods on route in the Binding the Nation exhibit by following a Native American trail that postal carriers followed between New York and Boston. There aren't any signs to guide you. The only way to find

MAKE THE MOST OF YOUR TIME Call or ask about activities in the Discovery Center, near the statue of Ben Franklin, the first U.S. postmaster. Kids may play games, hear stories, and create crafts that reflect museum exhibits. For example, in March, kids might study an Irish immigration stamp and make shamrock wands. In April, they often create hats to wear for Earth Day, and June might see them making flags to celebrate Flag Day. Come early for the best selection of materials.

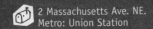
2 Massachusetts Ave. NE.
Metro: Union Station

 Free

 Daily 10–5:30

 202/633-5555 recording, 202/633-1000 voice,
202/633-9849 TTY; www.postalmuseum.si.edu

 3 and up

the right route is to look for notches in the trees. After the trail, step up on a stagecoach and play postal worker in a railway car.

In addition to all of the neat stuff here, the museum houses a collection of stamps. By pulling handles on vertical glass files, you can see foreign stamps organized by country, and U.S. stamps organized by date, from 5- and 10-cent stamps of 1847 to the latest issues. And if kids get curious about collecting stamps (a popular hobby for kids 100 years ago), they can create their own online collections and e-mail them home.

When you're ready to leave the museum, be sure to pick up a postcard. You can mail it to anywhere in the world from the little post office in the museum!

If you like this sight, you may also like the National Geographic Museum (#33).

KEEP IN MIND
While this museum helps give kids an appreciation for the postal system, they might like to know that camels, birds, reindeer, and dogs have all helped deliver the mail. Although Owney the Dog never carried any, he was still the mascot of the railway mail service in the late 19th century. Thanks to taxidermy, you can actually see Owney at the museum.

EATS FOR KIDS Gettysburger Address (cheeseburger) and Federal (chicken) Fingers are on the kids' menu at the **Capitol City Brewing Company** (2 Massachusetts Ave. NE, tel. 202/842–2337), in the same building as the museum. Across the street, you can find restaurants and more than 35 food stands offering everything from pizza to sushi at **Union Station** (50 Massachusetts Ave. NE). One of the best eateries is **America** (*see* D.C. Ducks #57), with suitably American regional fare. **Johnny Rockets** (tel. 202/289–6969), a 1950s-style hamburger joint, also appeals to families.

Known more for political animals than real animals, Washington nevertheless possesses one of the world's foremost zoos. Start with any must-see creatures on your child's list. On busy days there may be waits at the popular animal houses, such as the Giant Panda House, Reptile Discovery Center, or Amazonia's tropical rain forest. In the Flight Room, birds fly unrestricted. Orangutans swing on overhead cables from the Great Ape House to the Think Tank, where you can get a good look at the big apes while they get a better look at you. High-tech orangutans communicate with researchers using touch-screen computers.

Set among waterfalls, rocks, and bamboo grooves, the Asia Trail is home to red pandas, Asian small-clawed otters, sloth bears, clouded leopards, and the zoo's most popular residents. If your kid usually has his ears plugged with an MP3 player, he or she can go to the zoo's Web site and download an audio tour to use on the Asia trail. Adoring fans flock to the pandas, who come from central China. These playful, high-profile bears eat more than 50 pounds of bamboo every day.

EATS FOR KIDS
At the pizza playground next to the Kid's Farm, children can jump around on a huge rubber-surfaced pizza. When your tummies start to growl for a real bite to eat, check out the food kiosks, the **Mane Restaurant** on Lion/Tiger Hill or the **Panda Café** near—what else—the Giant Panda House.

MAKE THE MOST OF YOUR TIME
The Cleveland Park Metro stop is a better choice than Woodley Park/Zoo, with an uphill walk to the zoo but a downhill walk when you leave. Make sure your family wears comfortable shoes; the trek here is nothing compared to the walking you'll do over the zoo's 163 hilly acres. Rental strollers are available. Parking lots fill up in summer, so arrive early. In summer, early morning (or late afternoon) is a better time to catch animals alert; in cooler months, they're more active at midday.

3001 Connecticut Ave. NW.
Metro: Cleveland Park or Woodley Park/Zoo

 Free

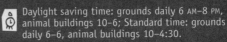
Daylight saving time: grounds daily 6 AM–8 PM,
animal buildings 10–6; Standard time: grounds
daily 6–6, animal buildings 10–4:30.

202/633–4800 or 202/673–0127;
www.nationalzoo.si.edu

 All ages

To see the world's fastest feline, check out the Cheetah Conservation Area. To see animals with anywhere from zero to eight legs, visit the invertebrate exhibit, where octopuses, nautiluses, and giant spiders dwell. If your child's idea of animals relates to lyrics with the letters E-I-E-I-O, check out the new Kids' Farm where you'll not only see animals that moo, neigh, cluck, and oink, you might get to help the zoo groom goats and miniature donkeys.

A trip to the zoo makes for an exhausting but fulfilling day. So that everyone emerges happy and healthy, pace yourselves; don't rush around trying to see everything. You can't. Stroll and enjoy what you do see. Watch your kids carefully; the biggest safety problem here is not animals but children wandering off.

If you like this sight, you may also like the National Aquarium (#38).

KEEP IN MIND Almost as ubiquitous as campaign bumper stickers in D.C. are stickers for FONZ (Friends of the National Zoo). If you visit and park at the zoo for more than four full days a year, FONZ membership pays off. In addition to free parking, you can also get discounts in the shop, go to camp, attend classes, and even spend the night at the zoo through Snore & Roar.

NEWSEUM

What is news? At this $450 million, 250,000-square-foot high-tech museum, you and your children can experience the story behind the headlines and even make some news of your own. Primarily funded by the Freedom Forum, a nonpartisan foundation dedicated to free press and free speech, this facility is a showcase for how and why news is made.

Fifteen theaters, 14 galleries, two high-definition television studios, touchscreen timelines, and more tell the story of the news—not only of today but also of yesterday and tomorrow.

Because a lot of news concerns war and death, some exhibits in the Newseum may be perplexing or inappropriate for young children. You can't necessarily predict when you'll come upon a graphic image, and screens constantly display today's news. It's best to provide guidance throughout the museum if your child is under 10 or is particularly sensitive.

MAKE THE MOST OF YOUR TIME In less than 20 minutes, a 4-D movie in the Annenberg Theater covers three journalists in three centuries: Isaiah Thomas reporting on the Battle of Lexington, reporter Nellie Bly going under cover at a mental institution, and broadcaster Edward R. Murrow reporting on the German blitz of London.

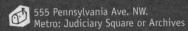 555 Pennsylvania Ave. NW.
Metro: Judiciary Square or Archives

 888/639-7386;
www.newseum.org

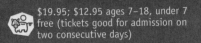 $19.95; $12.95 ages 7–18, under 7
free (tickets good for admission on
two consecutive days)

 Daily 9–5

 8 and up

Put your knowledge of the news into action. Through computers, your kids can experience what it's like to be a reporter or editor. They'll contemplate the ethics of anonymous sources and bias. Some questions may transfer to the lives of preteens and teens. For example as a reporter, you find out that your neighbor has been arrested. Do you tell your editor?

Or your kids might like to appear on camera, reading the news from a monitor in front of videos of the White House, the National Zoo, or the weather. Then you can download from the Newseum Web site!

Journalists are known for asking poignant questions and listening. After visiting this museum of news, your child should have a lot to talk about.

If you like this sight, you might also like the International Spy Museum (#48).

KEEP IN MIND
Extra! Extra! Read all about it! Don't let the ticket price deter you from visiting. Throughout the year (frequently on a three-day weekend), the museum hosts free, half-price, or other deals.

EATS FOR KIDS For a bite without leaving the building, try the **Food Section** on the concourse level. The cafeteria seats 152. But if you'd rather treat your future Katie Couric or Jon Stewart to a more formal meal try the **Source by Wolfgang Puck**. On the street level, the Source is a grill but upstairs it's fine dining.

OXON COVE PARK

If you want to take your children back to an era when taking care of the animals meant more than walking the family dog or feeding the cat, visit this working farm (also called Oxon Hill Farm) administered by the National Park Service. On a site where the Piscataway Indians once lived, this farm has animals and equipment typical of life in a bygone era—mostly the early 19th century and later.

Down on this farm you can find draft horses, sheep, pigs, ducks, geese, turkeys, cows, and goats—known as poor man's cows because they're capable of eating about anything and still producing milk and cheese. Many children's favorite animal is the milk cow who doesn't have horns. Unlike in the 19th century, most modern farmers stunt the growth of horns, as they're a hazard to farmers and other cows and they're no longer needed for protection.

KEEP IN MIND People often think that pigs are dumb, but some farmers believe they learn more quickly than horses and dogs. One popular conception that does hold true, however, concerns their trough manners. Watch as the cows' milk is delivered to them. Then ask your kids if they like pigs!

MAKE THE MOST OF YOUR TIME The farm gets the most visitors during the spring and fall when school groups come, but there's always parking and plenty of room for everyone to explore. Whenever you visit, remind your children to move slowly near the animals and not to make any loud noises or sudden motions. Such actions are likely to startle them. And though you will no doubt get a kick out of watching your child getting a kick out of the animals, also take a moment to appreciate the panoramic view of Washington over the Potomac River.

With supervision, your children can milk a cow, collect eggs warm from the nest, and toss corn to feed the chickens. Hayrides depart afternoons at 1:30, except on Friday, when they leave at 11.

A furnished parlor in a white farmhouse owned by the DeButts family in the early 1800s is open a few times each week. Park rangers and volunteers are usually on hand to talk about the British-born Mrs. DeButts and her views on slavery and the War of 1812. Call ahead to find out when kids can participate in daily chores and when the farmhouse is open.

Oxon Hill offers free, farm-fresh programs, including sheep shearing in May, cider making in September, corn harvesting in October, and "Talking Turkey" in November. Junior ranger programs in the summertime teach 9- to 12-year-olds about farm life. Reservations for all programs are a must.

If you like this sight, you may also like the Kids' Farm at the National Zoo (#24).

EATS FOR KIDS For fresh food, bring your own and take advantage of picnic tables in the shade near the parking lot, along the path to the farm, or near the house. A vending machine is stocked with water and juices, but no sodas. Otherwise, your options consist of fast-food outlets along Oxon Hill Road and the **Outback Steakhouse** (6091 Oxon Hill Rd., tel. 301/839–4300), a few miles away. Here kids can color and do crossword puzzles while they eat (or maybe so you can eat!).

What kind of noise does a bluejay make? How does a katydid sound? What about a beaver? Your kids are bound to find out. The first stop at the Patuxent Research Refuge is the Nature Calls kiosk: no spelling, reading, or typing is required to learn about the refuge's animals at this animated game in the lobby. But that's just the beginning as kids track down animals inside and outside this huge modern nature center.

Older kids might want to hang around Nature Calls to set up a rap session for birds, while younger kids may want to skip ahead to view Handles on Habitat, where they can pull a knob to see a pelican and osprey appear in the Chesapeake Bay or push a button to watch a scientist pop up with a mirror to look at birds' nests in the Hawaiian rain forest. Life-size dioramas of wild animals depict whooping cranes, timber wolves, and California sea otters swimming in kelp. The exhibits have enough buttons and knobs to amuse even toddlers.

EATS FOR KIDS Although picnicking is not allowed, on a pleasant day you may bring snacks to eat on the visitor center patio. Otherwise, the staff at the front desk can direct you to local fast-food restaurants, many of which are along Route 197. A 15-minute drive away in Laurel, **Pasta Plus** (209 Gorman Ave., tel. 301/498–5100) serves up homemade pastas, breads, and desserts, which you can also carry out.

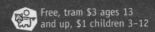
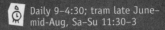

Patuxent hosts hunts, hikes, and activities for naturalists of all ages throughout the year. For example, preschoolers are advised to "dress to get dirty" for "Whacky Wetlands." Dragonflies of Patuxent is designed for kids 12-plus to learn how to identify these ferocious predators of the pond. The Kids Fishing Day held in early June attracts hundreds of anglers hoping for the big one.

You can take your own wildlife tour by following the well-marked trails. The paved Wildlife Loop is wide enough for a double stroller but short enough (about ⅓ mi) so preschoolers won't wear out. At the bird-viewing blind, even the youngest kids (with a boost from you) can peer through a slat as birds swoop within a few inches of their faces. Another 4 mi of trails, made of wood chips and other natural materials, satisfy junior and senior naturalists.

If you like this sight, you may also like Rock Creek Park (#19).

MAKE THE MOST OF YOUR TIME

On spring and fall weekends and daily through the summer, a 35-minute narrated tram tour runs through the refuge's meadows, forests, and wetlands, weather permitting. Though the narrator's commentary about wildlife management may be too advanced for your children, they probably will find the ride thrilling enough.

KEEP IN MIND You may be tempted to leave most of your cash at home because, with the exception of the tram ride, all activities are free. However, bring a little money for the Wildlife Images Bookstore, which sells some interesting children's merchandise at reasonable prices. Your children might like some stickers, rubber creatures, posters, or playing cards with pictures of endangered animals on them. Profits benefit the refuge.

PHILLIPS COLLECTION

This kid-comfortable museum, where you can sit back on a puffy couch or plop down on the carpet, was once the home—albeit the grand one—of Duncan Phillips, founder of the museum. In this home and in similarly scaled additions that retain the intimacy of a private residence, the museum features impressionists and modern American and European art. Six fireplaces and one fake fireplace (which looks real) add to the museum's homey feel. Unlike most other galleries, where uniformed guards appear uninterested in the masterpieces around them, the Phillips employs art students, many of whom are artists themselves, to sit by the paintings and answer questions.

The collection's best-known painting, Pierre-Auguste Renoir's *Luncheon of the Boating Party*, is particularly interesting to children because of its bright colors, the people engaged in happy conversation, and the terrier on the table. Kids can also relate to subjects like a ballet rehearsal, by Edgar Degas; a bullfight, by Pablo Picasso; and children playing hide-and-seek in a 19th-century house, by William Merritt Chase. Works by Swiss painter

KEEP IN MIND The Phillips Collection staff requests that everyone turn off their cell phones in the gallery. Also, keep a safe distance—12 inches—from all paintings and sculpture, because artwork can be damaged by accident.

EATS FOR KIDS You can purchase sandwiches, salads, and pastries at the **Museum Café** (tel. 202/387–2151 Ext. 351) in the gallery overlooking a courtyard. Open 10–4 Tuesday through Saturday and from 11 to 4 on Sunday, the café has booster seats but no high chairs. A better bet for a quick eat might be one of the many quick and inexpensive places to eat around Dupont Circle. For pizza, gyros, and other Greek concoctions made with tomato and cheese, try **Zorba's Café** (1612 20th St. NW, tel. 202/387–8555). At **Kramer Books and Afterwards Café** (1517 Connecticut Ave. NW, tel. 202/387–3825), you can buy a book and enjoy it with breakfast, lunch, or dinner.

 1600 21st St. NW.
Metro: Dupont Circle

 202/387-2151;
www.phillipscollection.org

 Donations suggested on
weekdays, $10 ($12 for
special exhibits) adult fees
on weekends, children 18
and under free.

 T–Sa 10–5, Su 11–6 (Su summer hrs
may vary), open Th until 8:30 PM

 5 and up, workshops
6 and up

Paul Klee also appeal to kids. His small-scale paintings include many kinds of symbols—even some that look like hieroglyphic symbols. But perhaps the artwork that will have the greatest impact is on the bottom floor of the museum's Sant building where works by local students through the Young Artists Exhibition Program are on display.

Gather a group of five or more kids (and call four weeks in advance) for a personal tour. The tour includes interactive activities led by the museum's enthusiastic education staff. If you don't have time to book an advance tour or if the idea of being with more than a couple of kids seems daunting, you can call ahead for a family fun pack (and impress your kids with your knowledge) or pick one up at the museum's entrance or download activity sheets from the Web site. Each pack includes artwork to discover, postcards or pictures, and activities you can try at home so the fun continues long after you've left.

If you like this sight, you may also like the National Gallery of Art (#34).

MAKE THE MOST OF YOUR TIME During the gallery's popular Family Free Days, held annually the first weekend in June, you can take part in projects (on a walk-in basis) that could entail anything from creative crafts and special tours to live music. Throughout the year, hands-on workshops for children and their parents ($15–$20 per adult-child pair) revolve around special exhibits and themes. Kids might find themselves at a photo shoot or making a sculpture.

ROCK CREEK PARK

On the biggest stretch of parkland in Washington you can truly take a walk on the wild side. Begin at the nature center, which brings the outdoors in. Upstairs, pelts, bones, feathers, and a bird's nest occupy a touch table near stuffed animals representative of the park. Preschoolers put on puppet shows featuring their forest friends in the Discovery Room. Downstairs, elementary schoolchildren use mice (the computer kind) to discover even more about the park's ecosystem. A 75-seat planetarium introduces youngsters to the solar system, and some shows include a Native American legend about a coyote that threw rocks to make pictures in the sky.

Take a hike on any of several trails near the center, but first pick up a discovery pack for each child at the front desk. Packs are equipped with binoculars, a magnifying lens, and a chart for recording the birds you see. The 15- to 20-minute Edge of the Woods trail, a flat, asphalt loop perfect for preschoolers and strollers, goes to a pond a little larger than

EATS FOR KIDS To wet your whistle, you can get a sip from the water fountain or purchase a bottle of water at the center. For anything else, you're on your own, but picnic areas are near the nature center. Pack a lunch from **Magruder's Grocery Store** (3627 Connecticut Ave. NW, tel. 202/237–2531), a 5- to 10-minute drive from the nature center. Near Magruder's are two inexpensive restaurants: **American City Diner** (5532 Connecticut Ave. NW, tel. 202/244–1949) and **Bread and Chocolate** (5542 Connecticut Ave. NW, tel. 202/966–7413), for those who want an elegant dessert. If your child doesn't care for éclairs or other pastries, don't worry; cookies are available, too.

5200 Glover Rd. NW; stables
5100 Glover Rd. NW (between 16th St. and Connecticut Ave., south of Military Rd.)

202/895-6070 nature center, 202/362-0117 stables; www.nps.gov/rocr/

Free; pony rides $20 for 15 min; trail rides $40 per hr

Daily sunrise–sunset; nature center W–Su 9–5; pony rides Apr–Oct T, W, Th 3 and 3:30, Sa–Su 1–3:30, trail rides T, W, and Th 6, Su 11–12:30

2 and up, pony rides 4–7, trail rides 12 and up

a bathtub. For older children, the Woodland Trail takes 40–60 minutes. On most weekends, rangers lead hikes on topics ranging from the lowly worm to the majestic wolf.

Take to the saddle: Rock Creek is the only place in town where kids can become urban cowboys and cowgirls (closed-toe shoes, preferably with a small heel, are required). Pony rides (reservations required) aren't just a trip around a circle; they're 15-minute rides through the woods. They'll take children as young as 2½ and as old as 11, but many preschoolers aren't ready for this excursion, and kids over 8 might find it babyish. On one-hour trail rides, guides take groups along some of the same wooded trails that presidents Martin Van Buren, Teddy Roosevelt, and Ronald Reagan and World War II general George Patton once rode.

If you like this sight, you might also like the United States National Arboretum (#9).

KEEP IN MIND

If your child is 6–12, ask for a Junior Ranger activity book. When your child completes at least six of the dozen activities, show the book to a ranger, so your youngster's hard work can be rewarded with either a badge that looks like the ones worn by park rangers or a Junior Ranger patch with a picture of a bolder bridge that goes over the Creek.

MAKE THE MOST OF YOUR TIME The planetarium offers free weekend shows at 1 for ages 5 and up (also on Wednesday at 4 for ages 4 and up) and at 4 for ages 7 and up. Children 4 and under may find the shows either boring or scary. (Before shows, the sun is shown setting over the Washington skyline; at the end, it rises and the room brightens.) At the end of the show, the rangers will give you a sheet showing the stars that you can see in the sky this month.

ROOSEVELT ISLAND

18

If the wildest animal your children ever want to see is a computer mouse, Roosevelt Island isn't for your family. But for kids who believe, as Theodore Roosevelt did, that "There is delight in the hardy life of the open," this sanctuary is a superb place to get away from the city's concrete, crowds, and cars. If it weren't for the airplanes from Ronald Reagan National Airport roaring overhead, you might forget you were in D.C. altogether.

The Island is a little tricky to get to as you'll need to be driving west on the George Washington Memorial Parkway. Leave your car in the parking lot next to the George Washington Memorial Parkway and walk over the bridge to this island wilderness preserve in the Potomac River. The 88.5-acre tribute to the conservation-minded 26th president includes 2½ mi of nature trails that crisscross marshland, swampland, and upland forest.

In the center of the island is a clearing, where a 17-foot bronze statue of Roosevelt stands, his right hand raised for emphasis. He is surrounded by shallow pools, fountains,

KEEP IN MIND How did the Rough Rider known for carrying "a big stick" inspire a stuffed animal? Once, when Roosevelt was hunting, his aides tied up an old bear for him to kill. But he couldn't shoot the defenseless animal, prompting a toy maker to create the teddy bear.

MAKE THE MOST OF YOUR TIME After you cross the bridge, you can see a large bulletin board where you can pick up a brochure with a map. Encourage your children to stay on the marked trails. Off the trails you may encounter poison ivy and great nettles, some as tall as 3 feet, better known as stinging nettles because you can feel a stinging pain if you rub against it. Gather a group of 10 or more people and call two weeks in advance to request a guided tour led by a park ranger, who will point out much more than where the stinging nettles are.

and four large stone tablets inscribed with his thoughts on nature, manhood, state (government), and youth. For example, he advised students at the Groton School in Massachusetts, "Keep your eyes on the stars, but remember to keep your feet on the ground." And there is plenty of ground for your feet to cover at Roosevelt Island.

To make the most of your visit, pack a backpack with some of the following items for your children: binoculars, a magnifying glass, a sketch pad and crayons or markers, a camera, and plant and animal guidebooks, if you have them. Cattails, arrow arum, pickerelweed, willow, ash, maple, and oak all grow on the island, which is also a habitat for frogs, raccoons, birds, squirrels, deer, and the occasional red or gray fox. But you won't see the animal most people associate with Roosevelt: the teddy bear.

If you like this sight, you may also like to see a memorial built in honor of Teddy's cousin Franklin (#54).

EATS FOR KIDS There's nothing to buy on this island—not even a soda. You may not want to drink too much anyway, because public restrooms close between late October and early April. The Park Service requests that you don't eat too close to the memorial, and there aren't any tables so you'll want to bring a blanket if you plan to picnic. Listen to the music of birds and the planes overhead as you eat.

Imagine your children making an animal paperweight or drawing animes while learning about ancient art techniques, geography, or other cultures. It's all part of the ImaginAsia program. Armed with guidebook and pencil, children (and their parents) search for ceramics, sculpture, and paintings and then go beyond simply writing about what they see. They may locate on a map where a work or an artist is from, interpret works, describe how they feel, or even invent stories. Afterward, you all meet in an education room, where you and your kids can create a take-home craft related to the exhibits seen. The program is operated on a drop-in basis, but it's usually best to arrive on time, as seats fill fast; reservations are only required for groups of eight or more.

Even if you're not visiting on a program day, there's plenty here to interest your kids. Activity-filled guidebooks are available at each museum's information desk. And just why are there two Asian museums, you might be wondering? The Freer Gallery, which contains one of the world's finest collections of Asian masterpieces, was endowed by Charles Freer, who insisted

MAKE THE MOST OF YOUR TIME Guidebooks list activities for a broad range of ages and abilities. Parents of young children will need to work with their kids to decide what's appropriate. Most children 10 and up can probably decide for themselves which activities are suitable.

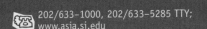 Freer: 12th St. and Jefferson Dr. SW; Sackler:
1050 Independence Ave. SW; Metro: Smithsonian

 Free

 Daily 10–5:30

202/633-1000, 202/633-5285 TTY;
www.asia.si.edu

 2 and up, ImaginAsia 6–14

on a few conditions: Objects in the collection could not be loaned out, nor could objects from outside the collection be put on display. Because of the latter, the connected Sackler Gallery was built. Like the Freer, the Sackler focuses on works from throughout Asia, but it also mounts visiting exhibits.

The Freer's collection also includes works by American artists influenced by Asia. One such was Freer's friend James McNeill Whistler, who introduced him to Asian art. On display in Gallery 12 is Whistler's Peacock Room, a blue-and-gold painted dining room, decorated with painted leather, wood, and canvas and, as the name implies, devoted to peacocks. Freer paid $42,000 for the entire room and moved it from London to the United States in 1904.

If you like this sight, you may also like the National Museum of African Art (#31).

EATS FOR KIDS

For restaurant choices, see any of the listings for museums on the Mall: the Castle, Museum of the American Indian, National Air and Space Museum, National Gallery of Art and Sculpture Garden, National Museum of American History, and National Museum of Natural History.

KEEP IN MIND While you're in the Peacock Room, think about the real peacocks that used to live at the gallery. In 1993 a peacock named James and a peahen named Sylvia resided in the museum's courtyard. After one year, the gallery needed to find a new home for the birds because Sylvia laid too many eggs. James and Sylvia lived with a farmer who loved them because they squawked to alert her when visitors arrived.

SIX FLAGS AMERICA

Washington is known for its educational and economical attractions. Six Flags America, the capital area's only theme park, isn't educational or economical, but it's exciting. Actually a combination theme park and water park (dubbed Hurricane Harbor), it contains more than 100 rides, shows, and games spread over 150 acres in suburban Prince George's County.

On the "dry" side, roller-coaster revelers have seven fast choices. The Wild One is a more-than-85-year-old classic wooden coaster. Roar mixes old-fashioned wood and modern computer technology to produce a thrilling ride. The four steel coasters are Batwing, Superman-Ride of Steel, the Mind Eraser, and the Joker's Jinx. Coaster traditionalists prefer the jiggle and clackety-clack sounds of the "woodie." Metal coasters follow a more circuitous route, with corkscrew turns and 360-degree loops. If your youngsters aren't tall enough (all rides, including the coasters, have height restrictions), to Thomas Town, named after the famous tank engine, for designed for the 6 and under set.

KEEP IN MIND To maximize your chances of minimizing expenses and aggravation, plan ahead. Look for coupons online or at grocery stores, or consider a season pass, which includes discounts at other Six Flags parks. If your child needs a stroller, bring your own to save the rental fee.

MAKE THE MOST OF YOUR TIME Lines form on weekends before the park opens. To avoid crowds, go on Monday or Tuesday, and make a plan on arrival, doing first what most interests your kids. If you're spending time at Hurricane Harbor Water Park, plan on getting out of your wet swimsuits a bit early. The "wet side" closes one hour before the park does.

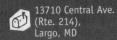

13710 Central Ave. (Rte. 214), Largo, MD

301/249-1500; www.sixflags.com

$49.99 over 54", $29.99 children 4 and up or 54" and under (add 10% entertainment tax); parking $15, 2 and under free

Mid-Apr–May, Sa–Su 10:30–6; Memorial Day–mid-June, M–F 10:30–6, Sa–Su 10:30–9; mid-June–mid-Aug, daily 10:30–7, Sa–Su 10:30–9 2nd wk in Aug 10:30–6, last week of Aug open only weekend. Labor Day weekend Sa–Su 10:30–9, M 10:30–8; Oct weekends only

2 and up

On the "wet" side, kids like Crocodile Cal's Caribbean Beach House. Water-powered activities here include a barrel that dumps 1,000 gallons of water on unsuspecting passersby every few minutes. The Hurricane Bay wave pool has a graduated entrance so even water babies (with parents, of course) can splash around, but an even better bet for little ones might be Buccaneer Beach. In a twist of the height restrictions, anyone over 54" must accompany a kid.

If you like this sight, you may also like National Harbor (#32), another attraction in Prince George's County, MD.

EATS FOR KIDS Approximately 10,000 pounds of sugar are used to make the roughly 100,000 servings of candy sold here each year—the same amount you'd use if you felt like baking nearly 1½ million chocolate-chip cookies. Like in other theme parks, food is expensive. If you bring your own, plan on eating outside of the park. No outside food is permitted, though you can bring in one sealed bottle of water per person. Vendors provide complimentary cups of water and ice. The **Johnny Rockets, Heritage House,** and **Crazy Horse Saloon** are air-conditioned.

You've got a two-for-one visit here. Both the Museum of American Art and the National Portrait Gallery share space in this mid-1800s building. Both museums are part of the Smithsonian Institution.

The work in the Smithsonian American Art Museum emphasizes art, rather than the subject. This museum is the home of one of the largest collections of American art in the world, including craft and folk art that kids can relate to. Nearly 42,000 artworks span more than three centuries. At the National Portrait Gallery, the emphasis is on the subject. From presidents to sports heroes to military figures, they're here in some form, including photographs, paintings, sculptures, and drawings.

Even if the distinction between the two types of art is lost on kids, most will find James Hampton's art interesting. Ask your son what he would do with an empty garage. Ask your daughter what she would do with hundreds of rolls of aluminum foil. Check out what Hampton

EATS FOR KIDS You can pick up a premade sandwich at nearby **Cowgirl Creamery** (919 F St. NW, tel. 202/393–6880; www.cowgirlcreamery.com). This self-titled cheese shop has an educated staff that can help you find the perfect cheese while your kids are encouraged to name their stuffed cow. Or purchase a bite at the café in a courtyard serves American fare. Either way, the expansive, light-filled Kogard Courtyard is a great place to unwind.

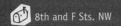 8th and F Sts. NW

 Free

 Daily 11:30–7

 4 and up

202/633–1000; AmericanArt.si.edu
or www.npg.si.edu

did when he was working as a janitor. For more than 12 years he built a huge throne using salvaged objects and what amounts to reams of silver and gold foils. His shiny *Throne of the Third Heaven of the Nations Millennium General Assembly,* referred to as the *Hampton Throne,* captivates kids of all ages. An unknown artist created *Bottlecap Giraffe* in the late 1960s. (No word on whether he or she drank all the sodas to get the caps.) Another artist, Nam June Paik, created a piece called *Electronic Superhighway: Continental U.S., Alaska, Hawaii,* using 343 televisions.

The Portrait Gallery has the only complete collection of presidential portraits outside of the White House. Ask your kids to find the sculpture of the president playing horseshoes.

If you like this sight, you may also like the sculpture gardens at the National Gallery of Art (#34).

KEEP IN MIND At the front desk, ask for a Portrait Discovery kit, which includes everything kids need to create their own self-portrait, write a label, and even compare it with a portrait of a doll. The Smithsonian American Art Museum offers free art programs once a month, usually on the second Saturday. Activities might include chalk drawing on the sidewalk, making baseball cards, and painting on canvas.

MAKE THE MOST OF YOUR TIME

The two museums share the Lunder Conservation Center on the third floor, where you can see the techniques used to examine, treat, and preserve artwork. If a conservator isn't at work when you arrive, you can watch a 40-foot media wall that shows them at work.

SULLY HISTORIC SITE

As at other local historic sites, kids can get a real feel for how people lived two centuries ago at this museum dedicated to life in the Federal Period (1790–1820). Your children may pretend to wash dishes in an old stone sink, cool off with a folded fan, or use sugar nippers. They may soak up the scent of the green and black teas that were popular at the time or get a whiff of No. 7, a cologne that George Washington (and more recently John F. Kennedy) wore. But kids also learn that life wasn't so sweet then, and not just because the early 1800s lacked our modern amenities. Slavery, too, is addressed, and your children can handle replicas of the passes that slaves needed to leave the property or lift the heavy cast ironware used in the kitchen.

Sully was the understated 1794 country home of Richard Bland Lee, uncle of Confederate general Robert E. Lee; his wife, Elizabeth Collins Lee; and their children. As Virginia's first representative to Congress, Lee cast one of two swing votes that put the nation's capital in his backyard.

KEEP IN MIND Some of the stairs in the Sully mansion are steep, so make sure unsteady toddlers, unsteady grandparents, and distracted parents are extra careful. Strollers are not permitted in the house, but the first floor is wheelchair accessible.

MAKE THE MOST OF YOUR TIME At least one weekend each month, Sully hosts special events. For example, Father's Day is the car show, the Sunday after Labor Day is the quilt show, and the first Saturday in November Sully celebrates Colonial Day. Admission may be up to an additional $4 during special events but there's more to do and see.

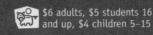

Purchase tickets and even souvenirs in a one-room log schoolhouse that was used in nearby Haymarket during the early to mid-19th century. In this tiny room, about a half-dozen children probably studied under a teacher who lived above the classroom.

Guides, often Fairfax County Park Authority volunteers, conduct one-hour tours of the Lee house on the hour. If the guides don't point it out, challenge your child to find the white squirrel in the parlor. When the Lee children were living here, their pet white squirrel was let loose in the house! On request, the guides may tailor their talk to your family's special interests (textiles or cooking, for example). Weather permitting, there is also the Forgotten Road Tour of the outbuildings, including reconstructed slave dwellings, at 2 (early March–mid-November). Most spring and summer weekends are especially festive, with such special events as quill pen writing, biscuit baking, and children's games.

If you like this sight, you may also like the Children's Museum of Rose Hill Manor Park (#62).

EATS FOR KIDS In the little schoolhouse you can purchase candy sticks, a treat that kids have enjoyed since the 1800s, and other candies. In summer, they also sell ice cream. For a meal, you have lots of options on Route 50, including **Cici's Pizza** (14392 Chantilly Crossing La., tel. 703/961–9100), an all-you-can-eat place, and **Five Guys Burgers and Fries** (14421 Chantilly Crossing La., tel. 703/817–7718), which sells two things—burgers and hot dogs.

THOMAS JEFFERSON MEMORIAL

Many children and adults may be surprised to learn that Thomas Jefferson didn't list being president as one of his greatest accomplishments. When he appraised his own life, Jefferson wanted to be remembered as the "Author of the Declaration of American Independence, of the Statute of Virginia for religious freedom, and Father of the University of Virginia."

The memorial honoring the third president is the southernmost of the District's major monuments and memorials, four long blocks and a trip around the Tidal Basin from the Metro. Jefferson had always admired the Pantheon in Rome (the rotundas he designed for the University of Virginia and his own Monticello were inspired by its dome), so architect John Russell Pope drew from the same source when he designed this memorial. But even children who have never heard of Rome, not to mention Jefferson, can still enjoy one of the city's best views of the White House from the memorial's top steps.

KEEP IN MIND Every spring, Washington eagerly waits for the delicate flowers of the cherry trees to bloom (many of which are near the memorial). Park-service experts try their best to predict when the buds will pop—usually for about 10–12 days at the beginning of April. But regardless of when they flower, the two-week long National Cherry Blossom Festival (www.nationalcherryblossomfestival.org for dates and information) is celebrated with the lighting of a ceremonial Japanese lantern, fashion shows, and a parade. When the weather complies and the blossoms are at their peak for the festival, Washington rejoices.

Tidal Basin South Bank. Metro: Smithsonian

 24 hrs; staffed daily 9:30 AM–8 PM

 Free

 202/426-6841; www.nps.gov/thje

 5 and up

Inside the memorial a 19-foot bronze statue of Jefferson on a 6-foot granite pedestal looms larger than life. And just in case your children didn't take the National Park Service ranger recommendation to research Jefferson before visiting the memorial, they can learn about this Renaissance man by reading his writings about freedom and government on marble walls surrounding the statue. The whole family can take advantage of ranger programs offered throughout the day or ask questions of the ranger on duty.

An exhibit called Light and Liberty, on the lower level, provides highlights of Jefferson's life, a timeline of world history during his lifetime and a 10-minute video. When you've seen it all, you and your children can judge for yourselves what Jefferson's greatest accomplishments really were.

If you like this sight, you may also like the Lincoln Memorial (#45).

MAKE THE MOST OF YOUR TIME

Allow about five hours to tour the monuments in Washington. From mid-April through November, you might want to set aside an hour for a paddleboat ride in the Tidal Basin (1501 Maine Ave. SW, tel. 202/479-2426; www.tidalbasinpeddleboats.com/). You can see the dock from the Memorial.

EATS FOR KIDS Rumor has it that some critics called the memorial "Jefferson's muffin" based on its shape. A short drive away in East Potomac Park is **Potomac Grill** (110 Ohio Dr. SW, at Maine Ave., tel. 202/554-7660), where you can get bran, corn, and banana muffins in addition to jumbo burgers and sandwiches at more reasonable prices than most Mall vendors. There's also a minigolf course there.

UNITED STATES BOTANIC GARDEN

Follow your nose. Or your eyes. Or your sense of humor. Or just follow the meandering paths around the amazing conservatory here. It's full of gardens to delight the senses and tickle the fancy with exotic, strange, rare, and beautiful plants from all over the world.

George Washington, Thomas Jefferson, and James Madison imagined a national botanic garden. Congress established the garden in 1820, the first greenhouse opened in 1842, and the conservatory was completed in 1933. This national treasure, the delight of botany lovers big and small, is more magnificent than the founding fathers could have imagined.

Kids can see plants that dinosaurs might have munched on in the Garden Primeval. Look down at the pathway for footprints from baby and grown-up dinosaurs. To learn how plants grow to become today's products, from fragrances to food, head to the Garden Court. See how bananas grow upside down from 20-foot stalks. Then check out the therapeutic uses of the specimens in Medicinal Plants.

KEEP IN MIND Read the signs carefully. With the exception of the Children's Garden, kids should not touch plants unless the staff invites them to feel a particular one. Allow at least an hour to see what's in bloom when you visit and to plant some seeds of wisdom in your own little gardeners.

EATS FOR KIDS If you bring your own picnic, you're welcome to sit out on the terrace in the summer or at the First Ladies Water Garden. For ice cream and other foods, check out the eateries under the United States Capitol, the National Museum of the American Indian, the National Gallery of Art, and the National Air and Space Museum. On a pleasant day, bring your meal over to Bartholdi Park, across Independence Avenue from the Conservatory. Frédéric Auguste Bartholdi, designer of the huge historic fountain, is best known for designing the Statue of Liberty.

 100 Maryland Ave. SW.
Metro: Federal Center Southwest

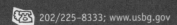 202/225-8333; www.usbg.gov

 Free

 Daily 10–5

 2 and up

In World Deserts, cacti grow sharp spines (some of which look like fishhooks) as protection from grazing animals, though of course they aren't in any danger here. A sign explains how cacti expand and contract like accordions. Children may not be as enchanted about orchids until they discover more about this diverse flowering family. For example, the beard orchid looks like it sprouted whiskers, and the mirror orchid attracts male wasps because its flowers look like female wasps.

To really dig in, head to the Children's Garden (open spring–summer), where children can try out gardening tools, meander through a tunnel made of bamboo, and hang out in a thatched roof cottage the size of a playhouse. Push the hand pump and watch a fish spout water into a fountain.

If you like this sight, you may also like the U.S. National Arboretum (#9).

MAKE THE MOST OF YOUR TIME If you'd like to chase a few butterflies or just need to get your child outside, take time to explore the National Gardens. The butterfly garden is just one attraction of this garden with native plants and a First Ladies Water Garden with a mosaic water fountain that you can dip your toes in. You can also enter the gardens from Independence Avenue or Maryland Avenue.

UNITED STATES CAPITOL

Throughout the Capitol, statues, paintings, and even the rooms themselves reveal much about the people and events that shaped our nation. The frieze around the rim of the Rotunda depicts 400 years of recognizable American history. Columbus's arrival, the California Gold Rush, and the Wright brothers' historic flight are all here. Eight immense oil paintings depict historical scenes, four from the Revolutionary War period. See if your child can find Pocahontas in the Rotunda. (*Hint*: She's in three places and she doesn't resemble Disney's cartoon.)

To tour the Capitol, you can book free advance passes through the Web site. Or you can take a chance that same-day passes are available at the Capitol Visitor Center's information desks. For passes to the chambers of the House and Senate, contact your representative's or senator's office. If the House Chamber looks familiar to your child, chances are you've let him or her stay up to watch the annual State of the Union speech. On the Senate side,

MAKE THE MOST OF YOUR TIME To take the 50-minute guided tour, plan for at least another 30 minutes of waiting and going through security. To enhance your children's experience, talk about Congress's role in our government and the Capitol's place in history before you arrive. Then during the tour, encourage them to move up front to see and hear better. Sometimes kids want to know how long it took to build the Capitol. The answer: 200 years and still building.

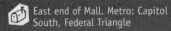 East end of Mall. Metro: Capitol South, Federal Triangle

202/224-3121, 202/225-6827 recording, 202/224-4049 TDD; www.aoc.gov; www.visitthecapitol.gov

 Free

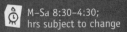 M–Sa 8:30–4:30; hrs subject to change

 8 and up

look for the sixth desk from the right in the back row. Since 1968, whoever occupies the desk keeps the drawer filled with candy.

Allow about two to three hours to tour the Capitol and its Visitor Center. Throughout the Visitor Center and National Statuary Hall, you'll find statues of people representing each state. Challenge younger kids to find statues of someone carrying a spear, a helmet, a book, and a baby. There's even a statue of a 7-year-old kid (Helen Keller). Tweens can look for statues of the person who invented television, a king, a physician, and a representative who said, "I cannot vote for war."

If you like this sight, you may also like seeing the other two big branches of government: the White House (#2) and the Supreme Court.

KEEP IN MIND
Keeping a secret was hard even before the Internet and cell phones. Statuary Hall was home to the House of Representatives 1807–57. Because of its perfectly elliptical ceiling, strange things happen to sound. A slight whisper spoken on one side of the hall can be heard on the other. On tour, try it. If the room isn't too noisy, the trick may work.

EATS FOR KIDS Even though it's rare to find them here, the restaurant in the Center has enough seats in the cafeteria for every member of the House of Representative and all the Senators. The 550-seat restaurant serves basic American fare from 8:30 to 4 PM. Sometimes, Senate bean soup is on the menu. This simple soup has been served in the exclusive Senate Dining Room every day for more than 100 years. You can try making your own with the recipe on the Senate's Web site (www.senate.gov).

UNITED STATES HOLOCAUST
MEMORIAL MUSEUM

Like the history it covers, the Holocaust Museum can be profoundly moving and emotionally complex, so you should first decide whether your children can appreciate it. The recommended ages published by the museum are guidelines only. During the busy tourist season (March–August), the museum is often crowded, making it difficult to obtain tickets (details below). The average visit is long, often 2–3 hours, and exhibits involve lots of reading. All that said, a trip here will be memorable for a preteen or teenager.

You don't need a pass for Remember the Children: Daniel's Story, an exhibit that tells the history of the Holocaust through the perspective of a young boy growing up in Nazi Germany. In this interactive exhibit, your children can follow events in Daniel's life. For example, they can see and touch his family's suitcases and clothing, and look into their ghetto apartment. At the end of the exhibit, kids are invited to write about their thoughts and feelings. It's a helpful outlet after this moving experience, which will be meaningful even for teenagers. You can then gauge whether to proceed to the main exhibition.

EATS FOR KIDS The museum's **café**, open 8:30–4:30, offers a variety of dishes, including matzoh-ball soup, kosher Asian-noodle salads, and even peanut butter and jelly sandwiches.

MAKE THE MOST OF YOUR TIME To avoid long lines from March through August, order advance tickets through the Web site. Ideally, it might be best for you to visit the museum without your children first to determine its appropriateness for your family. If that's not possible, consider going through Daniel's Story first.

The museum's main exhibition tells the story of the 11 million Jews, Gypsies, Poles, Jehovah's Witnesses, homosexuals, political prisoners, and others killed by the Nazis between 1933 and 1945. Striving to give a realistic first-person experience, the graphic presentation is as extraordinary as the subject matter: On arrival, each visitor is issued an "identity card" containing biographical information on a real person from the Holocaust. As you move through the museum, you read sequential updates on your card. The museum recounts the Holocaust through documentary films, videotaped and audiotaped oral histories, and a collection that includes such items as a freight car, like those used to transport Jews from Warsaw to the Treblinka death camp. Although there are four privacy walls to protect visitors from especially graphic images, they don't cover all that is horrific. After this powerful experience, the adjacent Hall of Remembrance provides space for quiet reflection.

If you like this sight, you may also like the National World War II Memorial, between the Lincoln Memorial (#45) and the Washington Monument (#6).

KEEP IN MIND Kids have shown they care and they will remember. More than 3,000 American schoolchildren painted their feelings on porcelain for the Children's Tile Wall on the lower level. They painted flowers, peace signs, clasped hands, many versions of the word "hope," and more in this moving tribute.

UNITED STATES NATIONAL ARBORETUM

How does your garden grow? Here the garden grows with priceless, 200-year-old trees smaller than a 2-year-old, herbs, an aquatic garden, and 15,000 magnificent azaleas. The arboretum has two entrances: New York Avenue and R Street, off Bladensburg Road. Whichever you choose, your first stop should be the administration building, where speckled, bright orange koi flourish in the surrounding pool. Some koi, also called Japanese carp, are as long as a child's arm, others as little as a finger. For a quarter, you can buy food for the fish and watch them swallow their pellets whole. Look for machines that look like they would contain gumballs. Pick up a map inside the visitor center. You'll need it. Almost 9 mi of winding roads cover 446 acres of botanical masterpieces.

Make sure you visit the National Bonsai & Penjing Museum. (In Japan artistic potted plants are bonsai and in China tray landscapes are called *penjing*.) These arts have been depicted in Chinese paintings as early as the 6th century. The idea is simple: Just as you get your hair cut to achieve a desired look, so these trees are trimmed for a desired look, which may vary by species. The trees are worth, "about as much as your children," according to the

MAKE THE MOST OF YOUR TIME You may drive, bike, walk, or do a little of each around the arboretum. If your kids bring their own wheels, there are even racks for locking bicycles scattered around. Driving is slow—the speed limit is 20 mph and enforced—but you can park at each garden/museum within the arboretum. There's a tram that runs on weekends and holidays, mid-April through mid-October ($4 adults, $2 children 4–16). The 40-minute ride may be good for older kids who are really into horticulture, but it doesn't make stops, so it's not ideal for an intensive look at the gardens.

curator. Many have been nurtured for generations, and some were gifts to presidents. Your children might enjoy wandering through outdoor rooms in search of the oldest trees, the smallest trees, or those with interesting trunks. Follow your nose to the National Herb Garden, where herbs from around the world are arranged. Kids can have fun figuring out whether the leaves of fragrant foods we eat really do smell. Look for oregano, wild strawberries, licorice, English lavender, and ginger. Dozens of heritage roses also bloom here. Fruits, vegetables, and flowers thrive in the Youth Garden, planted by school kids, who share what they grow with the homeless.

But plants aren't the only things jutting out from the earth. Twenty-two sandstone Corinthian columns that once stood at the east portico of the U.S. Capitol are set in a rectangle on a hill in a meadow.

If you like this sight, you may also like the Kenilworth National Aquatic Gardens (#47).

EATS FOR KIDS When you're ready to feed your children, don't be tempted to pick the fruits, vegetables, or herbs, no matter how delicious they appear. (Think the Garden of Eden.) A vendor serving drinks and snacks comes sporadically on pleasant weekends, spring through fall. Your best bet is to pack your own food and dine under the state trees or at tables with umbrellas on the terrace next to where the koi fish swim. As tempting as it might be for kids to feed the fish leftover crusts from sandwiches or even a carrot, the fish have a strict diet.

KEEP IN MIND Do you know your state tree? At the National Grove of State Trees, you can search for the official trees of all 50 states and the District of Columbia. Pick up a state tree list at the administration building. Don't look for markers on the ground; identification tags hang from the branches.

U.S. NAVY MUSEUM

8

This museum is a sure bet for any child interested in things military. Just call 24 hours ahead for a reservation and your kids can spin the wheels of sailing ships, peer through periscopes, and turn and elevate 40-milimeter long guns from World War II. All the while, they can get a maritime perspective on American history from the American Revolution to the present, including learning about the Navy's peacetime pursuits, such as diplomacy and humanitarian service. The U.S. Navy Museum is an especially good place to visit with a friend or relative who has served in the military.

Hands-on activities range from the no-tech, such as knot tying, to the high-tech, such as a Battle of Midway computer game in which children decipher coded messages. Free brochures listing activities for kids of all ages are available at the front desk. A kindergartner might do something as simple as draw a hat on a sailor or connect dots to make a plane; older kids are encouraged to search for a silver sailor created from dimes or write slogans encouraging military service.

MAKE THE MOST OF YOUR TIME On weekends, there's plenty of parking on base. On weekdays, there's a paid parking lot across from the 6th and M Street gate for visitors.

Washington Navy Yard, 11th and O Sts. SE
(weekdays); 6th and M Sts., SE (weekends)

 Free

 M–F 9–5; weekends and holidays
10–5; USS *Barry* M–F 9–5,
weekends and holidays 10–5

 202/433–4882;
www.history.navy.mil

 5 and up

If you call a few weeks in advance, you can arrange a special tour for your family or group. Themes include "Hats Off," during which kids learn about naval occupations by studying hats and then creating their own, and "To the Ends of the Earth and Beyond," in which middle-schoolers study the Navy's role in polar and underwater explorations.

Outside the museum your family can board the decommissioned destroyer *Barry*, a destroyer used during the Cuban Missile Crisis and the Vietnam War. Kids like the narrow halls, bunk beds, and mess hall, but they love taking the captain's wheel to "steer" the ship. Ahoy mates!

If you like this sight, you may also like the U.S. Navy Memorial across from the National Archives (#37).

KEEP IN MIND
If your children say they want to become sailors, tell them about the "powder monkeys." During the War of 1812, Mexican War, and Civil War, sailors—always boys, as young as 9—carried gunpowder from the magazine to the guns. It was a dangerous job, because these lads were often the targets of enemy fire.

EATS FOR KIDS During the week, dine in or carry out food from the Navy Yard's **food court** and familiar harbors **Subway** and **Dunkin' Donuts.** On weekends you have to bring your own meals. You can picnic any day of the week alongside seagulls at waterside picnic tables in the shade or sun.

VIETNAM VETERANS MEMORIAL

7

S ometimes kids ask some serious questions about war and death after visiting this moving memorial to the more than 58,250 men and women who died in Vietnam. Sometimes children think they're all buried at the monument. They aren't, of course, but the slabs of black granite inscribed with the names of the dead are as somber, as powerful, and as evocative of poignant reflection as any cemetery.

Known as "the Wall," the memorial is one of the most visited sites in Washington. Conceived by Jan Scruggs, a former infantry corporal who had served in Vietnam, these black granite panels that reflect the sky, the trees, and the faces of those looking for names (and perhaps crying when they find them) were designed by Maya Ying Lin, a 21-year-old architectural student at Yale. The nontraditional war memorial was originally decried by some veterans, but with the addition of a flagpole just south of the Wall as well as Frederick Hart's statue of three soldiers, most critics were won over.

EATS FOR KIDS Grab a hot dog or hamburger at a **food kiosk** behind the nearby Korean War Veterans Memorial.

MAKE THE MOST OF YOUR TIME Decode the symbols. Every name is preceded (on the West Wall) or followed (on the East Wall) by a symbol desig- nating status. A diamond indicates "killed, body recovered." A small percentage of names have plus signs, indicating "killed: body not recovered." Several hundred remains of men have been found and identified, so the symbols next to their names were changed to diamonds. If a man returns alive, a circle, as a symbol of life, will be inscribed around the plus sign. Alas, there have not been any circles added.

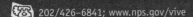 Constitution Gardens, 22nd St. and
Constitution Ave. NW. Metro: Foggy Bottom

 Free

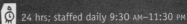 24 hrs; staffed daily 9:30 AM–11:30 PM

 9 and up

202/426–6841; www.nps.gov/vive

People's names appear on the Wall in the order of the date they died. To look up a name yourself, refer to the books posted at the entrance and exit of the memorial or ask at the white kiosk with the brown roof near the entrance. At the wall, rangers and volunteers wearing yellow caps can look up names and supply you with graphite pencils and paper to make rubbings of names.

Thousands of offerings are left at the wall each year. Although many people still leave flowers, remembrances have been evolving from personal objects such as letters from soldiers and clothing they wore to thank-you letters from school children.

If you like this sight, you may also like the World War II Memorial and the Korean War Memorial nearby. How does each memorial pay tribute to the soldiers who served? Encourage your child to talk with the park rangers at each site.

KEEP IN MIND Many people are surprised to learn that although 10,000 women served in Vietnam, only eight women's names are on the Wall. One of these is Mary Klinker, a nurse involved in Operation Baby Lift, a mission to bring Vietnamese orphans to the United States. Klinker's plane crashed in 1975.

WASHINGTON MONUMENT

Some kids say the Washington Monument looks like a giant pencil. Others think this 555' 5.9" obelisk (10 times as tall as its width at the base) punctuates the capital like a huge, partially buried exclamation point. Visible from nearly everywhere in the city, it's a landmark for visiting tourists and lost motorists alike and a beacon for anyone who yearns to shoot to the top and survey all of Washington below.

A limited number of free tickets, good for a half-hour period, are available beginning at 8:30 AM at the marble lodge on 15th Street, but on busy holiday weekends in the summer, lines may start forming at 7 AM. Advance tickets are available from recreation.gov. Arrive at the monument at the appointed time. Although lines to get in may be long, they move quickly. If your children are restless, have them count the flags surrounding the monument. Once you're inside, an elevator whizzes to the top in 70 seconds, a trip that originally took about 12 minutes in a steam-powered elevator back in 1888 when the monument opened to visitors.

KEEP IN MIND A lot of people are curious about the color change about a third of the way up on the monument. It took more than 50 years to build this monument. Fundraising began in 1833, and the cornerstone was laid in 1848. However, by 1854, construction had stopped and it didn't continue until after the Civil War with marble from the same Maryland quarries but of a different stratum and of a slightly different shade. At its completion, it was the world's tallest structure. It's still the tallest in D.C.

 15th St. and Constitution Ave. NW.
Metro: Smithsonian

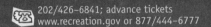 202/426–6841; advance tickets
www.recreation.gov or 877/444–6777

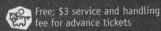 Free; $3 service and handling
fee for advance tickets

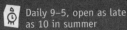 Daily 9–5, open as late
as 10 in summer

 5 and up

Each of the four sides has two viewing stations, and every other station is equipped with a step. Small children may think Washington looks like Legoland. Older children may enjoy trying to find Washington's landmarks. On a very clear day, you can see Shenandoah National Park to the west.

When you're ready to land, descend one flight of stairs to the elevator. This level also houses a small bookshop that carries a modest selection of children's books about Washington the place and Washington the man. After being up in the monument, take a good look at the top of the monument from the ground. Unlike a pencil lead (made of graphite), the monument is topped with a 7½-pound piece of aluminum, a very expensive metal in 1884, when the monument was completed.

If you like this sight, you may also like George Washington's home, Mount Vernon (#42).

MAKE THE MOST OF YOUR TIME Judging by the crowds, it seems there are as many people who want to look down on the Washington action literally as there are those who look down on it figuratively. If you don't want to wait in line, head to Washington National Cathedral's Pilgrim Observation Gallery (*see* #5) or the Old Post Office (100 Pennsylvania Ave., at 12th St. NW, tel. 202/ 606–8691).

EATS FOR KIDS
You can't take anything up with you, but a refreshment stand sells ice cream in summer and hot chocolate in winter, and sandwiches year-round. For some down-to-earth good food, *see* the restaurants listed for the United States Holocaust Memorial Museum and National Museum of American History.

WASHINGTON NATIONAL CATHEDRAL

Boys and girls go Gothic at this, the sixth-largest cathedral in the world. Like its 14th-century counterparts, the National Cathedral (officially Washington's Cathedral Church of St. Peter and St. Paul) has flying buttresses and 100-foot vaulted ceilings that were built stone by stone. Fanciful gargoyles adorn the outside of the building. The Cathedral is Episcopalian, but it's the site of ecumenical and interfaith services.

You can pick up a printed family guide at the information table at the west end of the Cathedral. A stained-glass window with an encapsulated moon rock celebrates the *Apollo 11* space flight, and the flags and seals of all 50 states can be found here. Kids also like counting the pennies in the floor of Lincoln Bay, and some visitors leave food for the poor at his feet. A charming children's chapel tantalizes the imagination with depictions of real and imaginary animals. Kneelers depict the story of Noah's ark. Or if you have a lot of time, see how far you get counting the pieces of stained glass that make up the West Rose window. There are more than 10,500!

MAKE THE MOST OF YOUR TIME Although the cathedral is a cool place for kids, it's still a house of worship, so encourage children to be as quiet as, well, church mice, in the main church and chapels. If they need to let off steam, take them to the Bishop's Garden, ideal for hide-and-seek.

EATS FOR KIDS The only place to eat on the cathedral grounds is the **Cathedral Store** (tel. 202/537–6267), which has sandwiches, snacks, and yogurt in a self-serve refrigerator. The cathedral is surrounded by gardens that are great for a picnic, however. A few blocks north you can find **Cactus Cantina** (3300 Wisconsin Ave. NW, tel. 202/686–7222), a lively Mexican restaurant where President George W. Bush and Laura Bush dined, **Cafe Deluxe** (3228 Wisconsin Ave. NW, tel. 202/686–2233), which includes a three-vegetable entrée among its children's offerings, and **2 Amys** (3715 Macomb St., tel. 202/885–5700), known as the best gourmet pizza place in the city.

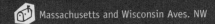 Massachusetts and Wisconsin Aves. NW

 Free; $5 donation suggested

 M–F 10–5:30, Sa 10–4, Su 1–4; may be open later hrs in summer

 202/537–6200, 202/537–2934 Family Programs; www.nationalcathedral.org

 4 and up, Medieval Workshops 5 and up

Hidden from view on the south side of the Cathedral, the English-style Bishop's Garden looks like the setting of the classic children's book *The Secret Garden* by Frances Hodgson Burnett. Boxwoods, ivy, tea roses, yew trees, and an assortment of arches, bas-reliefs, and stonework from European ruins provide a counterpoint to the cathedral's towers.

Brave boys and girls can ascend the 333 steps (many on a spiral staircase) to the top of the cathedral's central tower. The tower climb is usually only open once or twice per year.

If you like this sight, you may also like the United States Capitol (#11).

KEEP IN MIND At the east side of St. Peter's tower, almost at the top, is a stone grotesque of Darth Vader. A 13-year-old boy won a contest to design a decorative sculpture for the cathedral. Bring binoculars. They make Vader—and a lot of the other gargoyles—easier to spot.

WASHINGTON NATIONALS

4

Baseball fans have much to cheer about in D.C. In 2005, baseball returned to the District after a 33-year break, and then in 2008 when a brand new stadium was built with attendees, players, and the environment in mind.

Despite its long hiatus, professional baseball enjoys a long and rich history in our nation's capital that extends back to the late 19th century. The very first professional team in D.C. was the Olympic Baseball Club of Washington in 1871. A team called Capital Cities from the League of Colored Baseball Clubs arrived in 1887. There was a huge African-American following of the game in the District. From the late 1930s through World War II, the Homestead Grays, perhaps the greatest Negro League team ever, ran the bases here.

The Nationals, unofficially nicknamed the Nats, are represented by a group of young adults called the Nat Pack that revs up the crowd and helps give away goodies that kids love—T-shirts, pizzas, and magnets. On Sunday after the game, kids take to the field for the Diamond

KEEP IN MIND Washington, D.C., is also a mecca for youth soccer. If your kids get a kick out of this international sport, consider cheering on the D.C. United Soccer team (202/587–5000; www.dcunited.com), which plays at nearby RFK Stadium. One of 18 MLS (Major League Soccer) teams in the country, D.C. United has won more major national and international championships than any other U.S. team in history. Plays are called in both English and Spanish. Arrive early on weekends to participate in free speed kicks, dribbling contests, and other activities just for kids outside the stadium.

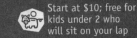
Start at $10; free for kids under 2 who will sit on your lap

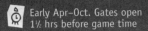
Early Apr–Oct. Gates open 1½ hrs before game time

1500 S. Capitol St. SE. Metro: Navy Yard

202/675-6287; www.nationals.com

4 and up

dash. The team's mascot, named Screech, predictably is an eagle, but some folks think he looks more like a chicken!

If your kids are more interested in Screech than in the game, a kid zone to the left of the entrance combines playground equipment geared toward 3- to 8-year-olds with activities for older siblings including a video arcade and cages for batting and pitching. Kids who really love Screech can make their own through the Build-A-Bear franchise.

Be sure to be in your seats for the fourth inning, when 10-foot-tall caricatures of the presidents on Mount Rushmore take to the field in the middle of the inning. Who will win? Washington, Jefferson, Lincoln, or Teddy Roosevelt? Find out at the game.

If you like this sight, you may also enjoy another local team, Bowie Baysox Baseball (#66).

MAKE THE MOST OF YOUR TIME

You don't need to search for a changing table here. All the restrooms are equipped.

EATS FOR KIDS You can munch on classic ballpark fare such as hot dogs, chicken tenders, and peanuts, but you can also order Kosher, Chinese, and Chesapeake Bay cuisine. You can also bring your own food (check the Web site for certain restrictions) or get carry out at the **Bullpen** across the street (1299 Half St. SE; www.thebullpendc.com), where the food is cheaper, but the pitching games and beanbag toss for tots may make it hard to leave.

WHEATON REGIONAL PARK

All aboard! A little red replica of an 1863 train chugs along on 10-minute tours through the woods at this park within 10 mi of D.C. But there's more for children here than just choo-choo rides.

Youngsters can whiz around on a carousel, ride a life-size statue of a camel, or peer over the turrets of a castle in a sandbox that can accommodate a whole class of kids. The playground is packed with bouncing wooden bridges, ladders, swings, mazes, wooden jeeps with bright plastic steering wheels, and straight and spiral slides in all sizes—from less than 6 feet long to more than 60 feet long.

Facilities for sports lovers include hiking trails, an ice rink, tennis courts, baseball fields, and basketball courts. The Brookside Nature Center offers dozens of free and low-cost nature programs throughout the year, including hikes, puppet shows, workshops, and summer camps, but even without a special program, the nature center is a fun place to visit.

EATS FOR KIDS
Picnic tables are scattered throughout the park. If you're planning for a crowd, consider renting a picnic shelter (tel. 301/495–2525; www.parkpermits.org), where you're guaranteed a dry place to eat, rain or shine. **Westfield Wheaton** (11160 Viers Mill Rd., tel. 301/946–3200), about 3 mi away, has a food court.

MAKE THE MOST OF YOUR TIME
If you're closer to the Potomac, you might prefer the 528-acre Cabin John Regional Park (7400 Tuckerman La., Rockville, MD, tel. 301/299–0024). Your child can swing, slide, and climb on playground equipment or watch the Bethesda Big Train baseball team (tel. 301/983–1006; www.bigtrain.org) play in a summer league. Facilities here also include a train replica that takes children through the forest and alongside the playground, where kids often wave to the train passengers. Feed trash to "Porky," the talking pig near the train station.

2000 Shorefield Rd., Wheaton, MD; Brookside nature center 1400 Glenallan Ave.; Brookside Gardens 1800 Glenallan Ave.

 301/905–3045, 301/962–1480 nature center, 301/962–1400 gardens; www.MontgomeryParks.org; www.brooksidenature.org; www.brooksidegardens.org

 Free; some attractions charge

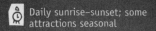 Daily sunrise–sunset; some attractions seasonal

 6 months and up

Kids can check out live snakes, fish, and turtles; play nature games on the computer; and put puzzles together.

Next to the nature center is Brookside Gardens, where formal seasonal displays of bulbs, annuals, and perennials and a sprawling azalea garden flourish outside, and seasonal displays and exotic tropicals blossom inside. Butterflies from North America and Costa Rica roam freely indoors at the Wings of Fancy exhibit from early May through mid-September. The garden's annual children's day held on the third or fourth Saturday in September features activities, crafts, and games.

If you like this sight, you may also like the United States National Arboretum (#9).

KEEP IN MIND You won't see Santa or a menorah at Brookside's Garden of Lights but you will see bears, owls, squirrels, cherry trees, and black-eyed Susans—all lit up brighter than stars to enchant children of all ages and all faiths. Many local families make this light show a holiday tradition. For a decent parking space on weekends, be sure to arrive early.

WHITE HOUSE AND VISITOR CENTER

It's extraordinary and fortunate that the most famous house in America is still open to visitors. You can see the place that President Dwight Eisenhower called "a living story of past pioneering, struggles, wars, innovations, and a growing America," but it takes advance planning: You can only tour with a group, you'll need to gather a group of 10 or more, and you must make arrangements to tour through a member of Congress. To visit in January, a month might be sufficient notice, but to visit in spring or summer you'll need to request possible dates about six months in advance.

Tours last about 20–25 minutes and take you through the East Room (where Teddy Roosevelt allowed his children to ride a pony and where the Jonas Brothers surprised Barack Obama's girls), the Green Room, the Blue Room, the Red Room, and the State Dining Room (where Bill Clinton's daughter, Chelsea, hosted pizza parties).

If you don't get tickets to the White House, there's another place to learn about our country's most famous house without having to harass your congress member—through its visitor

MAKE THE MOST OF YOUR TIME Are you ready to roll? Kids have been rolling eggs on Easter Monday on the White House lawn since the 1800s. But unlike previous generations, you can't just show up that morning and expect to participate. You'll need luck or connections. In 2010, more than a quarter million went online to request tickets. Less than 10% got tickets. But it's worth a try to be able to say that your children played at the president's house!

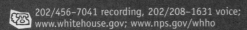

center where a video tour of the house continually plays and you can see photos. Challenge your child to find the gingerbread house, the pet pony named Macaroni, and the family prankster who ate all the strawberries intended for a state dinner and the gingerbread house. Just as if you were touring the actual White House, you can't bring in any food or drink, even water, with you. But unlike the president's place, the visitor center has room to roam and rest (seats and benches), as well as restrooms and water fountains, which aren't available on the White House tour.

Children can share their opinions with the president by e-mailing president@whitehouse.gov or penning a letter. The First Family even has its own zip code: 20500.

If you like this sight, you may also like the U.S. Capitol (#11).

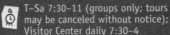

KEEP IN MIND The older your kids are, the more they can appreciate. The White House Visitor Center contains books, postcards, and educational games about the presidency and the White House.

EATS FOR KIDS At **Old Ebbitt Grill** (675 15th St. NW, tel. 202/347–4800), a Washington tradition since 1856, parents like the homemade pasta, and children like the choices on the kids' menu including grilled cheese and hot dogs. But if the idea of spending $6 for a kids' meal makes you cringe, try the food hall in the **Shops** (National Place, F and G Sts. between 13th and 14th Sts. NW, tel. 202/662–1200) for everything from greasy fries to gourmet salads at more reasonable prices.

WOLF TRAP NATIONAL PARK
FOR THE PERFORMING ARTS

Over a stream and through the woods, you can find a clearing with benches and a stage where Wolf Trap and the National Park Service sponsors Theatre-in-the-Woods for at least seven weeks every summer. Though Wolf Trap is most often associated with adult concerts, as many as 800 people per performance come here to see professional children's performers, such as jugglers, musicians, clowns, storytellers, and puppeteers.

Afterward, romping through the park is encouraged. Children (and parents) roll down the grassy hill and picnic in the meadow under shady trees. Sometimes park rangers give impromptu nature tours after the performances. Rangers may point out Virginia's state tree (the dogwood) and bird (the cardinal). They may also talk about how the bark and roots of the sassafras tree were used not only to make perfume, soap, and medicine, but also to flavor root beer.

For one weekend in September, Wolf Trap hosts the International Children's Festival, which features performers, crafts, and music from other countries. Many of the entertainers

KEEP IN MIND If you want to come back and see a performance at night, you'll have more than 100 to choose from between the outdoor Filene Center and the indoor Barns at Wolf Trap. If you choose to bring your children to the outdoor arena, the lawn is a wonderful place for families to stretch out and picnic on blankets.

MAKE THE MOST OF YOUR TIME Shows often sell out so if your child really wants to see a certain performance or you want to introduce your child to an art (opera, for example), pick up tickets in advance at the Filene Center or call Ticket.com (tel. 703/218–6500). On Tuesday, Thursday, and Saturday after the 10 AM shows, performers stay for about 40 minutes to teach workshops for children 5 and up. Groups of about 35 kids gain insight into the performing arts, learning puppetry, proper clown etiquette, simple ballet techniques, or mime moves. Reservations are a must for the free workshops.

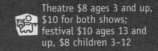
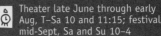

are children, yet previous guests have included clowns from Ringling Brothers and Barnum & Bailey's circus, and Bob McGrath ("Bob" on *Sesame Street*) and his big yellow pal. Three stages—the Theatre-in-the-Woods, the Meadow Pavilion, and the Filene Center (a covered amphitheater)—feature entertainment from puppet shows to dances. Kids who want their faces or wrists painted can choose from more than the usual animal or flower—they can select a flag from one of the countries celebrated or a U.S. flag.

Everything except food is included in the price. If it rains, everything moves to tents and the Filene Center but this doesn't dampen spirits too much.

If you like this sight, you may also like Glen Echo Park (#52).

EATS FOR KIDS No food or drink (except water) is permitted in the theater, because of bees and animals that might want to nibble your lunch. If you bring food, you'll have to keep it securely wrapped in a squirrel-proof container (think hard plastic instead of paper) during the show. For evening performances at Wolf Trap, whether you bring your own food or buy from their vendors, you're welcome to stretch out on the lawn.

CLASSIC GAMES

"I SEE SOMETHING YOU DON'T SEE AND IT IS BLUE." Stuck for a way to get your youngsters to settle down in a museum? Sit them down on a bench in the middle of a room and play this vintage favorite. The leader gives just one clue—the color—and everybody guesses away.

"I'M GOING TO THE GROCERY STORE..." The first player begins, "I'm going to the grocery store and I'm going to buy . . ." and finishes the sentence with the name of an object, found in grocery stores, that begins with the letter "A." The second player repeats what the first player has said, and adds the name of another item that starts with "B." The third player repeats everything that has been said so far and adds something that begins with "C," and so on through the alphabet. Anyone who skips or misremembers an item is out (or decide up front that you'll give hints to all who need 'em). You can modify the theme depending on where you're going that day, as "I'm going to X and I'm going to see . . ."

FAMILY ARK Noah had his ark—here's your chance to build your own. It's easy: Just start naming animals and work your way through the alphabet, from antelope to zebra.

PLAY WHILE YOU WAIT

NOT THE GOOFY GAME Have one child name a category. (Some ideas: first names, last names, animals, countries, friends, feelings, foods, hot or cold things, clothing.) Then take turns naming things that fall into that category. You're out if you name something that doesn't belong in the category—or if you can't think of another item to name. When only one person remains, start again. Choose categories depending on where you're going or where you've been—historic topics if you've seen a historic sight, animal topics before or after the zoo, upside-down things if you've been to the circus, and so on. Make the game harder by choosing category items in A-B-C order.

DRUTHERS How do your kids really feel about things? Just ask. "Would you rather eat worms or hamburgers? Hamburgers or candy?" Choose serious and silly topics—and have fun!

BUILD A STORY "Once upon a time there lived . . ." Finish the sentence and ask the rest of your family, one at a time, to add another sentence or two. If you can, record the narrative—and you can enjoy your creation again and again.

GOOD TIMES GALORE

WIGGLE & GIGGLE   Give your kids a chance to stick out their tongues at you. Start by making a face, then have the next person imitate you and add a gesture of his own—snapping fingers, winking, clapping, sneezing, or the like. The next person mimics the first two and adds a third gesture, and so on.

JUNIOR OPERA   During a designated period of time, have your kids sing everything they want to say.

THE QUIET GAME   Need a good giggle—or a moment of calm to figure out your route? The driver sets a time limit and everybody must be silent. The last person to make a sound wins.

BEST BETS

BEST IN TOWN
International Spy Museum
Mount Vernon
National Air and Space Museum
National Museum of American History
National Zoo

BEST OUTDOORS
Wheaton Regional Park (gardens and nature center)

WACKIEST
D.C. Ducks

GROSSEST
National Museum of Medicine and Health

COLDEST
National Harbor's ICE!

BEST CULTURAL ACTIVITY
National Gallery of Art and Sculpture Garden

BEST MUSEUM
National Museum of Natural History

SOMETHING FOR EVERYONE

ART ATTACK
Corcoran Gallery of Art, **59**
Hirshhorn Museum and Sculpture Garden, **49**
National Gallery of Art and Sculpture Garden, **34**
National Museum of African Art, **31**
National Museum of Women in the Arts, **26**
Phillips Collection, **20**
Sackler Gallery/Freer Gallery of Art, **17**
Smithsonian American Art Museum and the National Portrait Gallery, **15**

CULTURE CLUB
National Museum of African Art, **31**
Sackler Gallery/Freer Gallery of Art, **17**

FARMS AND ANIMALS
Claude Moore Colonial Farm, **61**
National Aquarium, **38**
National Zoo, **24**
Oxon Cove Park, **22**
Patuxent National Wildlife Visitor Center, **21**
Rock Creek Park, **19**

GOOD SPORTS
Bowie Baysox Baseball, **66**
Mystics Basketball, **41**
Washington Nationals, **4**
Wheaton Regional Park, **3**

HISTORIC HOUSES
Children's Museum of Rose Hill Manor Park, **62**
Frederick Douglass National Historic Site, **53**
Glen Echo Park, **52**
Mount Vernon, **42**
Sully Historic Site, **14**
White House and Visitor Center, **2**

LOST IN SPACE
College Park Aviation Museum, **60**
Goddard Space Flight Visitor Center, **51**
National Air and Space Museum, **40**
National Air and Space Museum's Steven F. Udvar-Hazy Center, **39**

ALL AROUND TOWN

MANY THANKS

This book is dedicated with appreciation to the museum guides, naturalists, docents, and volunteers who make Washington such an enriching environment for children. On a personal note for helping me to witness Washington's wonders through the eyes of children, I am grateful to my sons, Norman and Tim, and their nine cousins, Anastasia, Brady, Diana, Eddie, Erin, Kate, Mary, Matthew, and Owens.

—Kathryn McKay

the end.